THE REALITY
OF OUR
GLOBAL FUTURE

To Charlotte, Erin and Isla

each girl so young that she has virtually no past – only a future

and, as ever, to Francis

by far the most important part of my future

Dr Peter B Scott–Morgan

The

REALITY

OF OUR

GLOBAL

FUTURE

How five unstoppable High-Tech trends will
dominate our lives and transform our world

ISBN-13: 978-1470115487

ISBN-10: 1470115484

CONTENTS

Chapter 2 NETWORKING
SECOND-STAGE BOOSTER **58**

Chapter 3 MINIATURIZATION
THIRD-STAGE BOOSTER **100**

Chapter 4

SIMULATION

FOURTH-STAGE BOOSTER **134**

Chapter 5

ACHIEVING ESCAPE VELOCITY

IGNITION OF FIFTH-STAGE BOOSTER **176**

For I dipt into the future,

Far as human eye could see,

Saw the Vision of the world,

And all the wonder that would be...

Locksley Hall, Alfred, Lord Tennyson, 1835

PREFACE

Since the early 1980s, a succession of confidential clients has invited me to decode how different components of the world economy and the international community *actually* work and interact. For all that time I have had the privilege of being granted unique access around the world to a complete cross-section of the corporations, institutions, government organizations, secret groups, associations and informal societies that together make up the global community. It has been an extraordinary eye-opener.

Based on so much confidential insight into the hidden inner-workings of such a wide-ranging sample of the world economy, I was encouraged to write a book (now co-published alongside this one) about *The Reality of Global Crises*. However, it soon became clear that – urgent and topical through such subject-matter was – it only represented the more-threatening conclusions from my work. It explained why, in terms of global systems, there are so many apparently good beginnings that are nevertheless ending badly and leaving world-leaders increasingly powerless. But there was insufficient space in one book to detail exactly what the *good* endings were that those selfsame systems would generate provided we handled the threats well enough.

That was a shame because they are outcomes that are really worthwhile striving for: As you will find in this book, if only we can avoid the worst risks then, far from Global Chaos, many of us will instead get to experience an almost unimaginably spectacular *Global Renaissance*.

Peter Scott-Morgan
Torquay, 2012

HIGH-TECH overview

Our future will progressively be dominated by the counterintuitive impacts of five exponential trends that together form a High-Tech supertrend

- Exponential growth is easy to understand in theory but almost impossible to comprehend in practice

- Unlike most science fiction, it is the interaction of counterintuitive exponential trends that will dominate the future – which is why so much futurology is wrong

- High-Tech comprises five mutually-reinforcing trends – Digitization, Networking, Miniaturization, Simulation and a brand new entry – and they are all explosively exponential

DIGITIZATION...

...NETWORKING...

...MINIATURIZATION...

...SIMULATION...

...?

THE FIVE-STAGE LAUNCH ENGINE

HIGH-TECH

An arm's reach
or the orbit of Mars

Exponential growth is easy to understand in theory
but almost impossible to comprehend in practice

MOST OF US alive today will live to see something so extraordinary, so
monumental, so counterintuitive that it is almost incomprehensible. Yet,
maybe because it *is* so difficult to get our heads around, there has been no
serious public debate about it, no coordinated political action. As a result,
most people are left unaware of just why it is that a handful of nerdy-
looking trends is set to dominate everyone's lives and transform our world.

The largely-hidden mechanism behind this inexorable takeover is
actually pretty straightforward to illustrate. Imagine you are stretching
apart two markers – the further apart they are the greater the complexity
of a single computer chip at any given date. The first integrated circuit was
manufactured in 1958 so you can start in 1960, just as The Beatles are
forming, with your markers 1mm apart (that is about $1/25^{th}$ of an inch). By
1961 your markers are 2mm apart. By 1962 they are 4mm apart. 1963 it is
8mm. This is all comfortably slow. By 1965 your markers are still only
32mm apart – just over an inch. Acceleration at this rate everyone can
comprehend. But it is all about to go counterintuitive.

By 1970, only five years later when The Beatles have just broken up,
your markers are already a meter apart (more than a yard). In memory of
the Fab Four, if you visualize standing at the entrance of The Cavern in
Liverpool where they used to perform and keeping one of the markers
beside you, then by 1975 the second marker is on the other side of the
street, by 1980 it is thirty seconds' stroll down the road, by 1990 it is fifteen
minutes' walk away on the outskirts of town. By the Millennium
celebrations it will take you about an hour by cab to reach your marker.
Ten years later it will take you a few hours on a jet aircraft to reach your
second marker because it is already part way across the Atlantic. The
prototype chips currently in advanced development indicate that your

marker will reach John Lennon's memorial garden in the Big Apple in a couple of years' time.

Now see what happens if the complexity of computer chips continues to accelerate at that same rate. On page 31 you will see why that prediction is far *more* likely than many forecasters have assumed – but for now just accept it. You will need a virtual spaceship. If the predicted rate of growth continues, then your marker will reach the moon in less than a decade-and-a-half (by 2025). By 2040 you will be way past Mars and entering the asteroid belt.

EVERYTHING WITH CHIPS

After the initial prototypes of the 1960s, the figures that everyone quotes for the 'complexity of a computer chip' typically relate to the maximum number of transistors that could be built onto the most complex *yet still cost-effective* commercially available integrated circuit. By this measure, the trend of increasing-complexity has remained steady since the early 1970s, with the transistor count doubling every two years. There are already several *billion* transistors crammed onto a single chip. If this long-established trend continues, it implies by 2040 slightly more than a thirty-thousand-fold increase on today's figures, corresponding to approximately 150 trillion transistors on a chip.

That is from New York to Mars in less than thirty years. And yet after the first thirty years you could walk the distance between your markers in a quarter of an hour. And if from 1960 up to 2040 the markers had merely kept progressing at the same rate as they moved in the first year or so, then the distance they would have reached after the full eighty years would still be so small that you could move your finger from one marker to the other – by simply reaching out with one arm.

The difference between an arm's reach and the orbit of Mars is the difference between 'linear' and 'exponential' growth. Most progress is linear. The five trends that will dominate our future are all exponential.

FROM CORSETS TO TWITTER IN THREE QUICK DECADES

Unlike most science fiction, it is the interaction of counterintuitive exponential trends that will dominate the future – which is why so much futurology is wrong

ABSOLUTELY NOBODY HAS a gut-feel for what exponential growth is really like. We are just not wired for that sort of intuition. As human beings we are very good at comprehending trends that are linear – like a steady hill, the trend keeps climbing in a straight line. If we turn on the water to fill a bath and then leave the bathroom, with a bit of experience we can easily anticipate when to go back to turn off the water because we know the bath will fill at a steady rate. Likewise, if we are driving along the road at a fixed speed, we rely on the fact that in two seconds we will have moved twice as far as in one. That is the sort of prediction the human brain is intuitively amazing at. But we are terrible at imagining exponential explosions. When something explodes – not just gunpowder, but the popularity of a new toy, the number of people using the internet, a swine-flu epidemic – it is a fundamentally different type of progression: The larger something is, the *faster it grows even larger*.

That sounds as if it ought to be very simple to understand, and intellectually it is. If you are told that something will double every year (just as the number of transistors on the very first integrated circuits did for over a decade) you can easily handle the idea: after one year it will be twice, then after two years it will be four times, then eight times, then sixteen times and so on. Easy. It is only when it is pointed out that therefore after ten years it will be over a *thousand* times larger that the trend becomes a bit surreal. If someone then adds that after twenty years it will be more than a *million* times larger, it starts to feel absurd. Yet that is exactly the type of explosive growth that we are going to focus on throughout this book. And it is the exponential nature of the selected trends that makes the enormity of their eventual impacts on our lives difficult to grasp.

Even the more farfetched science-fiction stories based on the premise that It Is Possible So It Will Happen – the ones with flying cars and undersea cities – usually assume linear not exponential progress. The reason sci-fi writers tend to do that is not lack of imagination but because ironically it is only linear predictions of the future that feel intuitively believable to their readers. Most people (including politicians responsible for very-long-term planning) simply cannot handle exponential.

Yet despite the problems imagining it, the reality is that the changes over the next thirty years will be *inexorably exponential* because they will be dominated by the cascading explosions of everything from computer chips to available communication bandwidth to recording capacity to number of web sites. What is more, the progressive doubling will also force the *overall* rate of the international community's progress – just not as fast. The better the computers a biologist has access to, the faster the modeling that can be done of complex new drugs – so medical research will speed up. As will engineering. As will the rate of progress in science and technology generally. And modern architecture. And teaching. And new forms of the Arts. In fact, pretty well everything.

WHAT 'EXPONENTIAL' FEELS LIKE

It is, of course, very easy to get carried away. Many forecasters seriously underrate the role that psychological factors play in determining *which* aspects of society actually progress. Similarly, many scientists and technologists, as well as some politicians, tend to overestimate the rate of general progress because they *underestimate* the stabilizing impact of the past. I have taken all those factors into account. Yet despite the inescapable grip of the past and society's patchy adoption of new ideas, the fact remains that the rate of overall progress throughout the next few decades is nevertheless going to feel extraordinary.

When Queen Victoria was still on the throne, my grandmother was a young lady squeezed into a corset so tight she could almost place her hands around her whole waist. A lifetime later she told me that when she was a child she had believed the moon was made of cheese yet she had lived to watch astronauts walking on its surface – and that my generation would see as much change in our lives as she had in hers. She was slightly wrong. The likelihood is that we will see *vastly* more. She never sent a fax or left a voicemail or ever received unsolicited email – for her, spam was a form of processed meat. She never reheated something in a microwave oven, or tried to set the clock on a VCR. She never owned a CD collection, let alone downloaded a music track for her iPod. And she never captured a birthday party on camcorder, or looked for her cell-phone instead of searching for a clean public phone-box.

CHANGING THE DEFAULT FUTURE

Achieving change is relatively easy. What is difficult is substantially altering those changes from what will most-likely occur anyway. Despite what many chief-executives and politicians want to believe, it is actually surprisingly difficult to change the 'default' future – at least in a deliberate and substantial way. In practice, the future is kept remarkably stable because psychological factors combine with Legacy Effects (processes from the past that still tie into how today's world works so cannot easily be altered). If you think about it, without such relative stability our society would be so chaotic as to be almost impossible to live in.

She never paused a DVD to answer the door, or recorded something trivial using the miniature digital camera on her mobile, or relied on her Sat Nav to guide her through a complex set of road junctions. And she never accessed broadband internet to order groceries, check the weather forecast, make a free video-call to a friend in another country, or download a missed television program – each using a personal computer more powerful than the huge mainframes of the 1980s. All these things she missed. They only took off within the last thirty years. But the rate of those transformations in lifestyle that we all now take for granted is completely misleading. The next three decades will feel nothing like that.

They will be far more intense. Almost every aspect of the world economy will be revisited, reconceived, reborn. By 2040, even our most fundamental assumptions will be coming under scrutiny – what we consider to be 'thinking', or 'real', or 'mortal'. Yet, as highlighted in the final chapter of this book, throughout the 2020s and 2030s, the very genuine danger of major disruption will be ever-present. Progress has turned into something of a race against chaos. And for many it risks increasingly feeling like a full-blown revolution.

There is an unspoken truth about the exponential trends underlying the world economy. Even if everything goes as well as conceivably possible, the changes of the next thirty years will *not* be equivalent to the revolution in everyday-living seen since President Reagan and Prime Minister Thatcher were in power. They will be equivalent to the changes seen since Queen Victoria was in power.

THE SECRET HIDDEN IN FULL VIEW

High-Tech is driven by five mutually-reinforcing trends – Digitization, Networking, Miniaturization, Simulation and a brand new entry – and they are all explosively exponential

THE TRAJECTORY OF the global economy depends on a continuing cascade of immensely-long explosions. One of the most important of these first detonated over fifty years ago and triggered a chain-reaction that has been gathering pace ever since. The spread of its impact started small and was not even particularly noticeable for twenty years. Most people first felt its growing tremors during the 1980s as throughout the decade the great engines of the global economy powered up to full throttle.

Yet still today, with the global economy taking off and with the potential within another thirty years of it achieving escape-velocity into what could feel like a Global Renaissance, the escalating shockwave that increasingly propels it does not even have a name. 'High-Tech' is probably closest, and it has become a supertrend that dominates everyone's lives. It directly drives not just the progress of everything involving computers and electronics, but most of science and technology as well.

However, the term High-Tech does not even begin to convey its full nature. It is in fact made up of five largely-hidden exponential trends ingrained into the complex system called Modern Society. Each of these trends is so individually powerful that when they come together they generate the awesome propulsion of the High-Tech supertrend itself. Each of these five trends is inexorably driven by its own chain-reaction of explosive growth. But each is also so strongly reinforced by the others that together – as a supertrend – they are effectively unstoppable.

You might have thought that these five extraordinary drivers of global society would be obvious to everyone. Yet in reality they are so heavily camouflaged that people tend not even to recognize them for what they are. Their enormity fades into the background because during our day-to-day lives we are only aware of those parts of the supertrend that impact us directly. Things like upgrades in computers or mobile phones stand out. Others – such as developments in wafer-fabrication or communication protocols (let alone advances in molecular biology) – may not even register. But in fact they are all linked. We cannot see that they are each part of something far more complicated because the overall mechanism that drives them is lost within the complexity of society as a whole – a secret hidden in full view. Unintentionally, and over many decades, the five trends that make up the High-Tech supertrend have become encoded and buried within the inner-workings of the global economy itself.

Nothing indicates this better than the everyday-language used to describe them. There is none. Probably the most accurate terms (even though they sound overly technical) for the four out of the five trends that are most deeply established are: *Digitization, Networking, Miniaturization* and *Simulation*. Exactly why each of these labels represents something that is in fact of fundamental importance is what most of this book is about. Suffice to say now though, the very fact that merely to name these crucial trends it is necessary to resort to jargon shows just how very well-hidden the full scale of each one is, and how unrecognized their individual significance and contributions remain.

As a result, some implications for how the future will develop have previously been misinterpreted or underestimated – albeit they have nevertheless sometimes been very well publicized. In the remainder of this book I will try to correct some of those errors you may have already come across. But mainly, I will reveal the findings of what is the first-ever comprehensive analysis of the future that is solidly based on confidentially-obtained insights into the otherwise-hidden workings of the world economy.

FOUR ESTABLISHED BOOSTERS AND A NEW ONE

I will progressively build up a full picture of the next few decades by working in turn through each of the five exponential trends that together form the overwhelmingly-powerful High-Tech engine that is launching the world economy on a voyage into completely unfamiliar territory. Each trend is a powerful booster in its own right, but they are very-largely working together like a multi-stage rocket. And that is now of vital relevance to everyone – even to those numerous people who do not really care very much about High-Tech or world economics at all.

THE REALITY OF OUR GLOBAL FUTURE

How well the five boosters of the High-Tech launch-engine perform is no longer merely of direct relevance to scientists, politicians, economists and business people. It is equally crucial to those who are bored stiff by science, politics, economics and business. Our global economy is *already* taking off. We are all at extreme risk if it crashes. We are collectively unable to power down without catastrophe. Whether we are unaware of it, do not care about it, or even disapprove of it, we are *all* now committed to the launch.

Over the next couple of decades, each booster will further steepen the trajectory of the world economy – pushing the limits as it thrusts overall progress ever-upward on an exponential trend. At least for the moment. As I have already mentioned, as things stand our current trajectory just about allows the global economy to reach a form of 'escape velocity' by 2040 after which it breaks free from some of its current restraints (such as energy and complexity-solving ability) into a form of Global Renaissance. But there are no guarantees. If our trajectory over the next handful of years flattens too much, then our progress will not be fast enough to avoid all the turbulence that the economy's acceleration is stirring up.

In the five chapters of this book that correspond to the five-stage boosters of our collective progress, rather than make the typical futurology mistake of treating the trends as if they were in isolation, I will instead build the analysis of each successive trend on what came before – reflecting the heavy interaction between the trends that will inevitably occur in reality. In the first chapter, you will see how Digitization is on an almost-unstoppable course to creating a polarized society that has virtual-assistants, robot cars, cyborgs and everything on-the-record. In the second chapter you will see how Networking will combine with Digitization to lead by 2040 to computers capable of human-like interaction and an internet a *billion* times more powerful than today's. The third chapter reveals how the Miniaturization trend offers nanotech breakthroughs ranging from cancer treatments to quantum computing – but not, as has often been suggested, Star-Trek Replicators or 'grey goo'. And in the fourth chapter, you will see how exponential Simulation will support fundamental and sweeping advances that lead to almost limitless electricity and maybe almost limitless life-extension.

Finally, you will see how the backdraft of the High-Tech launch engine is stirring up a turbulence of unintended consequences that threaten to disrupt our trajectory so much that we can no longer outrun a growing onslaught of escalating global crises that risk eventually engulfing us. Rather than Global Renaissance we would then face Global Chaos. And yet, there is something extra. Out of that turbulence is also emerging a brand new exponential trend – which looks like placing a *fifth*-stage booster directly under the control of the general public. That includes you. It carries an implication though: For us to learn how to direct that power most effectively so as to give our world civilization the extra boost in the right direction that it needs, we must first understand just what the hidden forces are that are struggling to propel us toward such an extraordinary and liberating future. That is what this book is for. Certainly, the amazing future it reveals is a destination that we *could* miss. But it is also a destination that we truly *can* reach. And if we manage to get there, it will blow our minds.

Here is why.

DIGITIZATION overview

Digitization is on an almost-unstoppable course to a polarized society of virtual-assistants, robot cars, cyborgs and everything on-the-record

- Within decades everything will potentially be on-the-record, and personal Virtual Assistants will be needed to access a lifetime's data

- Digitization of a largely Analog world may be one of the most important transitions for the world economy in five-thousand years

- Robots will not turn out like in the movies but – especially in the forms of cars and tractors – they will be widespread within decades

- Many predictions that robotic technology will be used to enhance humans are misdirected – even for some proposed military applications

- The net effect of all the future impacts of Digitization will tend to polarize every aspect of society throughout the international community

INTELLIGENCE AMPLIFIERS...

...ROBOT PETS...

...EXOSKELETONS...

...NEVER-ENDING VIDEO DIARIES...

FIRST-STAGE BOOSTER

DIGITIZATION

A NEVER-ENDING VIDEO DIARY OF YOUR WHOLE LIFE

Accelerating capacities for digital-data storage means it will soon be affordable for members of the general public to record and keep non-stop videos of their lives

PERHAPS THE MOST common prediction about the technology of the future is that personal computers in a few decades will be like miniature versions of the supercomputers that exist today. That particular prediction is reasonably correct as far as it goes although, as explored on page 76, it is highly debatable whether the concept of any form of standalone computing device will even exist in a few decades' time. But leaving that to one side for the moment – and broadening the definition of 'personal computer' to include what today are thought of as mobile phones and Sat Navs – I can confirm that, based on everything that is currently happening in corporate research labs, the global economy is indeed on a trajectory to use computer-based devices that have better and better voice recognition, on-demand real-time language translation, cleverer ways of letting users interact with them, and above all that make an increasingly complex world *easier* to manage.

That last feature is deceptively important. Just think how many different operating instructions and passwords and user names and 'significant dates' we are currently forced to remember. And how to reduce the chances of ID-theft we are supposed to keep changing our access codes far more often than most people actually do. And how it seems that as soon as we learn how to program our latest alarm clock, or boiler, or TV recorder, or cooker – we have to learn how to program a new one. Even in today's world, a virtual assistant would help. In tomorrow's world it will be vital.

Only with each of us having our own virtual assistant will we run any hope of making sense of the mounting body of data at our disposal. The

Storage and access

fact that such an assistant will typically come complete with its own personality and voice and simulate a visual identity on screen will simply make it all the more natural to interact with. In many ways it will behave like a loyal and informed friend. But it is not just that without it we risk being overwhelmed by the ballooning amounts of freely available information – the public stuff at least will broadly be categorized to help make it accessible. The real problem will be making sense of the exploding *personal* archive that we each build up, off the cuff, unstructured, year on year.

Virtual Assistants and Intelligence Amplifiers

Accessing data archives will be so problematic that personal Virtual Assistants will be vital to retrieve the right data and in so doing amplify a person's capabilities

THE POINT IS that computer-storage costs are dropping exponentially, so for a lot of people it has already become the norm to archive many of their emails. There is simply no need to delete them, and it is sometimes useful to track back and find out what someone wrote – if only to look up a website address they mentioned. Within only a few decades, you will easily be able to afford to record, on a handheld camera contained within something like your mobile phone today, a video diary of *every second of your life,* and never have to delete anything. Every meeting, every conversation, every memory.

But that on its own is of little use. It is a bit like someone archiving every single email they ever receive into one long continuous document-file on their laptop, line upon line, in sequence, without any form of indexing – and then trying to find that specific website address someone sent. In practice, looking through an electronic video-archive is far worse even than that because there is no easy way of searching through moving images; there is currently no equivalent of a Keyword search for video.

For someone to access, automatically translate, and then print a transcript of the vaguely-remembered foreign newscast they could not quite follow when they watched it with a Chinese musician on a business flight to Los Angeles several years ago (or it *might* have been that she was a Japanese businesswoman and it was when the family was heading off on vacation) – that takes a really clever virtual assistant. But access to such support will change your life. And the lives of everyone who chooses to interact with you, never forgotten, always on-the-record.

Storage and access

This version of the future, in which everyday-people can each make practical use of a massive personal archive of recorded memories, is extremely likely. It is also world-shattering. That is not just because of the extraordinary potential it will provide for ordinary people to enhance their recall and interpretation of events. It is not even because every camera on every street and road, in every shop and office, within every communication device within every home, will itself potentially also always be recording – millions of public cameras already are today. The reason it is so radical is because the existence of virtual assistants will mean it will be possible to interpret those recordings automatically, recognize faces and voices, transcribe conversations, and react accordingly. Maybe even, upon occasion, reading someone's words back to them – against their will – in court – decades later.

THE SELF-FULFILLING PROPHESY

Since the 1960s many electronics experts have misinterpreted the systemic reinforcements that long ago turned 'Moore's Law' into a self-fulfilling prophesy

BUT HOLD ON a moment. There is a potential major flaw in the logic of everything you have so far read in this book. And it would completely invalidate all the predictions and would bring into question the relevance of any of the strategic implications. What if current technological trends simply do not continue for very much longer? After all, even skilled financiers relying on ever-rising house prices or informed politicians predicting a continuing boom in the economy all got their basic assumptions utterly wrong. It is a very reasonable concern. Indeed, many people – including a few claiming to be technological experts – simply do not accept the underpinning assumption that electronics will continue to explode for more than maybe another decade at most.

Therefore, how can I assume in my forecasts that computing power will continue to increase dramatically for several decades? Why should I confidently expect digital-storage costs to keep spiraling downwards? After all, no exponential trends can last forever. Surely, the High-Tech launch engine will inevitably soon throttle back. It is a vital set of concerns to address in detail up-front because otherwise everything else in this book should rightly remain suspect. But for you to understand why the hidden reinforcements within the Digitization trend are totally different to those affecting trends like house prices and GDP, you need to understand why in my early-twenties I rebelled against the judgment of some top-scientist colleagues.

In 1975, Gordon Moore (the co-founder of the semiconductor company Intel) refined an observation he had made ten years earlier about the growing number of transistors on a computer chip. He now said he expected that the number would double every two years – a prediction famously named 'Moore's Law'. Eight years later I was finishing writing a textbook due for publication in 1984. To put things in context, that was the year Torvill and Dean won a score of twelve perfect 6.0s for their Boléro in the Winter Olympics. It was the early period of Ronald Reagan and Maggie Thatcher. Band Aid recorded the original *Do They Know It's Christmas.*

In my book, and rather to the concern of my publisher, I stuck my neck out by claiming that the exponential growth-rate in computing-power of the early 1980s would actually last far into the future, despite the fact that several informed people were hotly debating whether that level of progress could possibly continue even throughout the 1990s. Prior to my book's publication, some expert reviewers complained to the publisher that I had completely underestimated the technical challenges – the computing trend was at best sustainable for another ten years.

They also claimed that even if it were theoretically possible to overcome the technological challenges, in practice there would not be sufficient demand from electronics manufacturers to justify the investment. After all, this was a time when most people had not the faintest idea of what a personal computer even was, let alone could conceive of one in something called a 'mobile phone'. In their recommendation to my publisher that I be required to delete my 'overenthusiastic' forecast before the book was published, my technical reviewers authoritatively stated that the manufacturing technology, let alone the investment needed for it, simply did not exist to sustain such an escalation. That was their irrefutable logic. They were each two or three times my age. They were top scientists. I thought they were missing a crucial insight.

COUNTERING THE EXPERTS

My logic went like this: 'Academics are presenting this as a prediction, but it is not. Gordon Moore is now Chairman and CEO of Intel. Intel is the world's largest semiconductor company. Moore's Law is not a prediction; it is a business-strategy. What is more, Intel is clearly so confident it can fulfil that strategy that it has told the world. As a result, every electronics and computing manufacturer who buys chips from Intel will develop new designs based on the assumption that in two years' time they will be able to get double the power on a chip.

'Meanwhile, all of Intel's competitors will think the same, so they will feel they at least have to match Intel in doubling the power of their own chips every two years. And the companies that design components for the increasingly sophisticated wafer-fabrication plants that make the chips will also gear up to this exponential rate. And software engineers will do the same. And the marketing departments. And the retail stores. And all of us.' My conclusion was that my reviewers were totally underestimating Moore's Law. It was not a prediction. It was not even just a strategy statement. It was *a self-fulfilling prophecy.*

What Moore had done was adapt a technique employed by charismatic leaders across the ages: If something is stated convincingly enough, others will act accordingly even if the logic is a little shaky. Intel very effectively changed the unwritten rules of what became the Information Technology industry by ensuring that it was in *everybody's* enlightened self-interest to do whatever was necessary to adhere to something that, in reality, was nothing more than a rather arbitrary historical phenomenon. Until that moment, the prediction could *in no way* be justified as being called anything other than perhaps 'Moore's Hypothesis'. But as soon as it became part of the hidden workings of the global economy, it did indeed become a Law worthy of the name. Those experts in the 1980s who concluded that the semiconductor industry would not rise to the major challenges ahead had only taken account of part of the equation. Like all-too-many of us scientists, they were logically very adept but *psychologically* less so. And they had missed what was really going on.

Experts being too close to their particular topics of expertise is actually a surprisingly common problem. That is because, however knowledgeable people are in a particular subject, if they do not also understand enough of the complex and often hidden inner-workings of society as a whole, then even as experts they can get confused about which growth rates in their field are stable and which are not. Combined sometimes with a little intellectual arrogance, that can lead them to make totally misguided professional judgments.

Back in the early 1980s I held my ground and eventually persuaded my publisher to leave my prediction intact. Almost thirty years later everyone now takes for granted the astounding sustained rate of growth in computing power over the last several decades. It did indeed stay exactly as it had been in the early 1980s. Yet fascinatingly, some people are *still* predicting the end of the exponential growth 'in about ten years' – using exactly the same logic as before. As you will see next, as we explore what is currently going on beneath the surface of the world economy, today's naysayers are *even less likely* than my 1980s reviewers to be proved correct.

BUILDING THE GREAT PYRAMIDS
ON A CHIP

The original reinforcing cycle behind the accuracy of Moore's Law has now turned into something far more relentless that is set to last for several more decades

THE ORIGINAL SELF REINFORCING cycle behind the accuracy of Moore's Law has now turned into something far more relentless. These days every part of every home and office in developed and developing countries is filled with integrated circuits. It is not just the obvious electronic gadgets like computers, televisions and audio equipment. It is nearly *all* electrical appliances – from dishwashers to telephones and from heating-control systems to burglar alarms. Then there are cameras. And personal audio. And up to half the cost of a high-end car can be its electronics. And that does not even touch on all the software that modern consumers use – including the incredible amount crammed onto high-definition digital televisions and called Movies or TV Shows. Of course, to record that resolution the TV companies needed to upgrade their cameras, and their editing equipment. In parallel, the broadcasting stations had to do the same.

As a result of these sorts of dynamics, there is hardly an industry left on the planet that is not directly or indirectly affected by the exponential growth in computer power. What is more, there are innumerable related technologies (memory, hard-disks, networks, displays) that also have exponential growth rates – some of them growing even faster than computer chips. And on top of all that, the *speed* of processing is also increasing. It is the compound effect of all of these related explosions interacting together that, more than anything else, dictates the trajectory of the High-Tech supertrend and all the associated incessant changes in modern society. It is ultimately what makes most of them possible.

DIGITIZATION

It is how supermarkets can handle their amazingly flexible inventories and keep their prices down. It is how Google and Amazon get better and better at finding us what we want. It is how consumers can now pay their bills over the phone during the evening giving verbal instructions to a computer. It is how special effects on film and television have become so good that many people no longer even realize that much of what they are watching is faked. These accelerating capabilities are now so firmly established – so fundamental to corporate business plans, so inextricably part of the lifestyle that everyone wants and expects – that the multiple exponential-growth rates powering the High-Tech supertrend have become woven into the very fabric of the world economy.

That type of embedding is actually far more common than most people recognize. There are many other aspects of global society that are also very deeply entrenched: the units people use for measuring time, the number of days in a week, city layouts, models of government, the notes used in music, computer-keyboard layouts, language. Although there are lots of specific details around why these all stay relatively stable, the overriding explanation is that in essence they have each become so interconnected with other aspects of society that it would cause unbelievable disruption if they ever did radically change – not least because of all the side-effects and unintended consequences that would result. As a result, they tend largely to remain as they are. This 'Legacy Effect' is a fundamental attribute of all human communities – from rural villages to corporate multinationals. Basically, the more that individual components of society become integrated, interconnected and interdependent, the more difficult it becomes to change them, let alone stop them. And that applies just as much to deeply-embedded long-term explosions such as Digitization.

OVERCOMING TECHNICAL CHALLENGES

The various exponential trends that characterize Digitization (computer-chip density, magnetic-disk capacity, network bandwidth, number of pixels, and so on) are all tightly interlinked. But they are also, as we have just seen, increasingly integral to almost every other aspect of global civilization and nearly every facet of the world economy. That is the main reason why the fifty-year-old chain reaction of Digitization is set to continue exploding for the foreseeable future – the trend is so tied into everything else that its basic characteristics are now almost unchangeable.

SPACE PSYCHOLOGY

The way that The Future evolves tends to be dominated not only by the legacies of the past but also by the group-psychology of the present. Leaders (along with futurologists) tend seriously to underrate the role that psychological factors play in determining *which* aspects of society actually progress. For instance, public support enabled the race to the moon to continue throughout the 1960s, but the loss of that support effectively shelved manned lunar-exploration for around half a century. What is more, given that conquering deep-space is technically far more challenging than exploring the deep-ocean, it might reasonably have been expected to see at least a few large undersea research-colonies established by now. But the public will almost certainly watch astronauts exploring the surface of Mars long before governments allocate similar levels of funding for aquanauts to live and work at the bottom of Earth's oceans – for no great logical reason other than simply that travelling to another planet is more likely to capture the general imagination. And the huge infrastructures of organizations like NASA have been around for so long that they are already very deeply intertwined into the workings of wider society. And pictures of bright planet surfaces look better on TV that ocean depths ever can.

With that said, even just to maintain Moore's Law alone, there are all sorts of extremely serious problems with the physics as electronics gets down to the incredibly small sizes of components that the continuing growth rate implies, not least issues of overheating. Indeed, as far as we can currently tell, it may not even be theoretically possible to continue using the same class of solution as we currently employ for more than a couple of decades. At best. But there are other ways. Fundamentally different ways. They are in research labs already, and I will explain some of them later.

When people warn that 'no exponential growth can last forever, and Moore's Law will hit a limit' they are, of course, completely correct. But there is still a very long way to go until progressive miniaturization means that Digitization gets down to the scale of atoms. And manufacturers can also go in the other direction and build bigger (and more three-dimensional) chips. And there are some seriously weird and wonderful things that can be done with the so-called Quantum Effects that occur at very-small sizes. Ultimately all these problems are 'merely' technical ones. Comparable, admittedly, to building the Great Wall of China, or the Pyramids at Giza, or a rocket that can take men to the moon and back. But when a lot of civilization's infrastructure is focused on challenges like that, humanity has consistently demonstrated that it is rather good at overcoming them.

THE OFFS AND ONS OF EVERYDAY LIFE

Computer-chip complexity in fact only indicates the maximum realistic speed at which the far-more-fundamental process of widespread Digitization can accelerate

A SIMPLE APPLICATION of Moore's Law alone cannot predict something like all-pervasive video-recording, any more than it can predict affordable wall-sized TVs, which are also very likely. That is because magnetic, optical and other recording media follow a largely distinct growth path to integrated circuits (far more separate, in fact, than flat-panel displays do). This highlights a major misunderstanding about Moore's Law. Even senior government advisors assume that it is the regular doubling of computer-chip complexity that ultimately will drive society's progress. But that is not really true. Although Moore's Law stands out so much, in reality it is like the highly-visible exploding volcano that accompanies an earthquake that sets off an undersea rockslide that creates a pressure-wave in the ocean that only much later as it approaches land finally becomes visible as it rears into a tsunami that will seem to appear from nowhere. Moore's Law is just a very-obvious explosion that everyone can see. In reality, there is something far more fundamental going on.

Only when you explore really deeply into how society operates, underneath readily-visible trends like 'conspicuous consumption' and 'consumerism', do you find a massive fault-line in the world economy that has been fracturing since long before the very first integrated circuit – and that without which Moore's Law could never even be possible. The international community is breaking with what for millennia has seemed like common sense. Human experience is of a world that is continuously changeable: Sounds can grow imperceptibly from silence to a deafening roar, a single note can continuously rise in pitch from a vibration to a whistle, and the length of a note is infinitely variable. In consequence, it is very natural for people to represent their continuously-changeable world by mimicking it with other continuously-changeable things that are analogous to the original (like paint-pigments are for colors in a rainbow, or the moving shadow on a sundial is for the passing of time). But in contrast to everything around them, technologists are now converting the world into something that either *Is* or *Is Not*. Global society is resorting to numbers – discrete, all-or-nothing, digits – as it rapidly shifts from Analog representations to Digital ones.

THE SILICON TAIL WAGGING THE HIGH-TECH DOG

It is a common assumption, even by top technologists, that it is the regularly doubling of computer-chip complexity that is at the very root of society's High-Tech progress. But just because a new computer chip comes out that is – roughly – twice as powerful as its predecessor should not of itself change anything in society. Why would anyone bother to buy one? Given that most of us already have personal computers and mobile phones that do their jobs perfectly adequately, why would we choose to get rid of them before they eventually stopped working – any more than we do with an expensive pen? And when we did eventually change them in ten or twenty years' time, why would we not simply replace them with near-identical models that did the same job and operated almost exactly as before – just as with domestic power-tools, sofas, beds, bicycles and gas cookers? When it comes to High-Tech, there is something far more powerful going on than just the availability of exponentially-more-complex chips.

A superficial explanation is that High-Tech manufacturers use the extra complexity to keep enhancing their products and then they exploit sophisticated marketing techniques to encourage subtle peer pressure that persuades the rest of us that we cannot live without the new upgrades. But if that were the full answer it still would not explain why the same does not occur with things like bicycles – even though modern manufacturing techniques would indeed allow steady enhancements at a fixed price provided enough people bought them. Instead of regularly-doubling computer power, it is the overall shift of society from Analog to Digital that is more truly at the root of our currently-exponential progress.

Analog to digital

At first glance, using digits to represent continuous things seems a bad idea. Most digital watches only tick off the seconds, whereas an analog watch with a continuously-sweeping second hand shows as many fractions of a second as you are quick enough to catch. What is more, it is always going to be easier to make simple mechanical calculators that are analog rather than digital. There were already remarkably sophisticated analog computers to calculate astronomical positions well-over two *thousand* years ago – as demonstrated by the example found in a wreck near the Greek island of Antikythera.

In contrast, the first designs for a mechanical digital computer were made less than two *hundred* years ago by Charles Babbage, and proved too complex to complete in his lifetime. But digital representations capable of being processed mathematically fit far better with *electrical* devices – even if those machines only use clunky electrical relays. There is little that is more clear-cut than the On or Off of electricity. And because any number can be encoded with a long enough sequence of only two binary digits (1 or 0), a combination of electrical Ons and Offs can in fact represent any value, any brightness, any volume – anything analog at all.

What is more, quite coincidentally, the On or Off states also conveniently match the Yes or No conditions of basic scientific logic (known as Boolean algebra). The combination of all these factors taken as a whole fit together extraordinarily well. Digital representation *and* electrical devices *and* binary notation *and* mathematical processes *and* Boolean logic are made for each other. Indeed, they turned out to be such a uniquely powerful combination that around the middle of the 20th century they sparked the genesis of the Digitization trend.

THE LURE OF DIGITIZATION

It sounds trivial, almost boring. In fact, the shift to Digital may be the most significant transition since populations first gathered into cities at the dawn of civilization five-thousand years ago. Although it was only in the mid-1970s that the self-fulfilling prophecy of Moore's Law began to kick in, it was already the pull from Digitization that actually *made it worthwhile* for everyone to be such willing accomplices.

It was becoming increasingly attractive to convert more and more aspects of the analog world into digital representations so as to handle them in ways that would otherwise be impossible. First documents, then music, pictures, video. Digital circuitry began to spread outside the realm of computing (even of 'home computing') and instead took over consumer electronics. Faster than any technological transition before, consumers replaced their record turntables and tape decks with CD players. But they only did so because their favorite music was now being digitized onto CDs. And that had an extraordinary impact.

RISE OF THE DIGITAL COMPUTERS

In principle, the Victorians could have built working electrical computers using relays – but they could never have made ones complex enough to compete with the technologies that followed. That is because, despite what people often think, the main difficulty with building a complex digital device using relays, or even the thermionic valves that replaced them in the 1940s, is not their size or the power they consume. It is their unreliability. Individual components keep breaking down. And if you make too complex a device then statistically at any time at least one component in your machine will be broken, so the whole will *never* work properly. As a result, decades before Moore's Law was established, the increasing lure of Digitization was already powering developments in digital computers. The hidden significance of the historical progression from relays to valves to transistors to integrated circuits is that at each stage they became vastly more reliable.

For the first time the general public all began to understand the benefits of Digitization. There was not any background hiss. Someone could even scratch a CD and it still played properly. And if they copied a CD, the copy was perfect – however many generations of copies they made. That encouraged even more Digitization using electronic stills-cameras, and scanners, and videocams, and mobile phones. Then consumers replaced their VCRs with DVD players. Soon after the start of the 21st century, worldwide digital storage capacity overtook analog capacity, and the Digital Age really got going. Today, digital storage capacity continues to grow exponentially. Worldwide it is currently estimated to have reached around one zettabyte (that is, a million billion megabytes). As all this occurred, people increasingly realized that they could handle digitized images, digitized sounds and digitized text in remarkably similar ways – even attaching them to emails. And then came Blu-Ray – so they could take full advantage of their new digital high-definition TVs.

DIGITIZATION IS STRONGER THAN MOORE'S LAW

If an unforeseen technological breakthrough suddenly meant chip complexity could double every year (rather than every two years as at present), the inexorable pull of the more-fundamental Digitization trend would still dominate and would still continue to encourage not just the development of ever-greater processing power but also greater recording capacity, higher pixel-resolution, broader communications bandwidth and all the other related developments not directly governed by Moore's Law at all.

Today, almost every archived analog recording of music on the planet has been digitized, as have more than one-in-ten films ever made, and one-in-twenty books. And the more that the international community has gone digital, the more attractive it has become for chip manufacturers to keep up with growing demand for devices to access and process all that digitized data – and to create even more material. That is the reality behind the deeply-embedded exponential growth of computer-chip complexity. Things like Moore's Law are themselves reflections of the far more fundamental trend of Digitization of the whole global economy. Despite what is usually claimed, Moore's Law has never in reality 'driven society's progress' – it has only ever indicated the *maximum realistic speed at which that progress can occur.*

How Accountants Rewrote the Future

Many predictions of future applications for robots have deeply underestimated the impact of accounting conventions as well as the costs of mechanical components

DIGITIZATION IS DRIVING the world economy toward far more than just extra-powerful computers. In fact, parts of the High-Tech future are utterly different to what Moore's Law alone predicts – not least because all of that computing power is going to stretch far into the physical world and directly interact with it in ways that are sometimes the very opposite to what people have been led to believe. Within twenty years, for instance, you will indeed at last get the chance to own a personal robot worthy of science fiction. But it is not going to look quite as you might think.

The robotics elements of the Digitization trend are not as cut-and-dried as some other aspects because they are strongly linked to fields such as mechanical engineering that are still in part developing independently of digital electronics. As a result, even robotics experts if they do not sufficiently understand how their field fits into the broader context of society as a whole can end up making predictions for a few decades' time that involve humanoid domestic robots and androids that care for the aged in their homes.

In reality, I am afraid that is not going to happen. As things stand, the first serious domestic robots will not look anything like C3PO – they will look far more like very large streamlined boxes on wheels. This is because of the often-unrecognized economic system in which robot development sits. Much of the cost of a robot is all the mechanical components. Although the computer bits get exponentially cheaper over time, all the moving parts largely continue to cost the same as ever. They may get a little less expensive the more the manufacturer makes, but they will never drop in price the way the computer-electronics will. As a result, robot bodies will basically always cost a lot.

The implication for advanced automation in general is that, for anything other than dangerous work, it is far more difficult to move robots out of the research lab than most people assume. Just because it is possible to make a prototype, does not make it economically attractive to use it. It is the same sort of mundane reason people will not all have flying cars in the foreseeable future – manufacturers could almost make them today, but the physics of keeping something airborne means that with any currently available technology they would simply cost too much to run.

NICE GRIPPER – SHAME ABOUT THE COST

With hindsight, it is no great surprise that the bulk of my original PhD research – which modeled the technical and managerial aspects of complex environments – ended up informing all the subsequent work of my career analyzing the hidden drivers of society. Far more surprisingly, even the impressive-sounding robotic 'Omnigripper' that I developed as a side-project (and rather optimistically was granted a patent for) carried a useful lesson. At the time I thought the design was rather clever; it was certainly mechanically very complicated. The trouble was that the moving components cost more than the whole computer I had dedicated to controlling them – and in the early '80s even a microcomputer cost a sizeable chunk of my PhD equipment-budget. In design terms that did not bother me, because I knew that over time the computing cost would drop like a stone. The problem, as with all robotic equipment, was that however much the electronics dropped in price, the cost of everything else would stay expensive. Today, as then, to manufacture the gripper's mechanical components a post-grad would have to budget the price of a reasonable second-hand car; in contrast, the same computing power that I then used would now hardly cost enough to justify filling out an expenses-claim.

The disconcerting truth is that many of the well-accepted forecasts about robotics are a bit shaky because the very technologists that governments and investors and journalists and the general public assume are most likely to make accurate predictions tend all to share a major blind-spot. The humdrum reality of how accounting conventions and capital-depreciation policies dominate the take-up of robots is something researchers typically ignore completely – it is a whole world that they (along with many politicians) often have no real intuition about.

The same is true of many of the journalists reporting those predictions. And those business people who *do* understand such economic realities, rarely have sufficient technological depth to take issue with the initial predictions. It is a pattern I have seen play out time and again: Some of the greatest errors in previous forecasts have been caused by a lack of 'joined-up thinking' across apparently separate topics that in reality are connected.

HUMANS VERSUS ROBOTS

In robotics, one of the most extreme examples of this is the way that the future impact of automation is heavily determined by, of all things, centuries-old accounting practices. For reasons of ease and habit, most public and private businesses as well as government departments justify buying a major piece of equipment by calculating how many years it will take for expected savings to pay-back the original investment – or they use various more-sophisticated calculations that are nevertheless broadly similar in intent. These are very widespread accounting approaches, and that means they will be very slow to change (the Legacy Effect, yet again). But all-too-often these approaches create a bias against adopting robots.

The reason is that fortunately most societies do not anymore buy human slaves outright in the way they buy equipment. Instead, people in effect 'rent' employees by the hour or by the month. As a result, standard practice is to account for the cost of *people* in a totally different way to equipment. So when it comes to deciding whether to use robots or people in a factory, or on a farm, or even at the office, it can all get a bit confusing. It often appears to accountants and bankers that it is more cost-effective to use people (who *in a given year* do not cost very much) rather than invest in long-lasting sophisticated robots (which initially cost a lot, even though over their long lifetimes they may end up cheaper than the total equivalent human payroll added up over all those same years). Reinforcing that bias, many manual workers who are not sure what other type of work they would do if they lost their jobs – together with their trade-unions and the politicians they potentially vote for – may not be too enthusiastic about robot replacements either.

THE POWER OF MONEY – AND OF HABIT

The technical consultants to Stanley Kubrick's deeply-researched *2001: A Space Odyssey* (filmed in the mid-1960s) knew that flat-panel displays and space-station hotels could both be available to the public by the early-21st century. Only one of them is – and that is because of cost-effectiveness, not availability of technology. And the clothes that people in fact wear today are closer in style to the fashions of the '60s than to anything predicted in the movie. That is to do with habit, not lack of imagination.

It is primarily for these reasons that, even in a few decades, many factories around the world will still be full of human workers performing tasks far below their capabilities even though, if accounting practices and employment issues were not a factor, robots and advanced automation would technologically be capable of replacing many of them. And yet, ironically, at the same time as many manufacturing bosses will still choose not to use robots in their factories, as private individuals they will be starting to buy immensely sophisticated robots for their own use.

WHAT YOUR FIRST SCI-FI ROBOT WILL *REALLY* BE LIKE

Although many expectations for robotics will be dashed, hugely sophisticated yet affordable robotic cars and tractors will be readily available to the public by 2040

THE MOST ACCURATE way to picture the best-selling consumer robots of 2040 is simply to imagine an ultramodern car. That is because actually they are very likely to *be* modified cars – driverless, talking, robotic family-cars than can operate on unmodified roads. And people will be able to afford them because, even today, there is so much of a modern high-end automobile that is *already* electromechanical that the extra parts needed to make it fully robotic will not cost a tremendous proportion more. Even today's drivers do not realize how much help they are getting from on-board computers (for everything from braking to traction control) to make their travel safer. Transitions to electric or hybrid cars will make robotic upgrades even more cost-effective. The end result will be safer, more energy-efficient, more luxurious, and in principle capable of being 'driven' by everyone from young children to the disabled – although for a long time regulation will probably insist that a licensed driver remains 'in control of the vehicle' at all times.

Eventually, whole lengths of highway (selected fast lanes on motorways are most likely to be first) will be allocated exclusively to robotic cars that, because they can communicate with each other, will be able to travel far faster and much closer together. Imagining how quickly people could get away from traffic lights if only everybody could be trusted to put their foot down simultaneously and all speed away as one, conveys the general idea of just how much more efficiently traffic can flow in Robot-Only lanes. Today's traffic jams are as much a function of human reaction-times as volume of traffic, so governments will far prefer to encourage more efficient use of existing roads than try averting gridlock by building hugely expensive new ones. And subsidies for robotic cars will be a likely incentive that will accelerate adoption still faster.

Naturally the research costs for all this will be high, but they can be spread over millions of cars. Within only around ten years from now, enhanced-vision systems for luxury cars will emerge that, for example, can penetrate fog (and then perhaps highlight kerbs by displaying them on the windscreen, cleverly monitoring the driver's eye-gaze direction so the windscreen-display accurately superimposes over the real-world view that the driver has).

At current rates, potentially-self-driving cars and vans on everyday roads will be commercially available by 2030 and common by 2040. At a minimum, in emergency situations these systems will take over, much as antilock breaking systems do today. And because large country-fields are far simpler to negotiate than main roads, fully-robotic agricultural tractors will become commercially available even earlier – although the relatively low volumes will mean that automotive manufacturers are most likely to use farm vehicles to prototype potentially fully-road-worthy systems planned for launch to the general public only a few years later. In principle, freight trains and then passenger trains could be fully automated much earlier than any non-rail transport. But in reality that transition will be slower than you might think. Safe automation of trains is already largely achievable but for a long time will continue to be blocked by unions and others raising concerns over safety. Commercial trucking is likely to follow a similar sequence, starting around the same time as robot cars are first introduced.

In contrast, today's ships and airplanes are already very highly automated. Unknown to most passengers, commercial planes often land without any direct intervention from the pilot. However, the deeply-established prestige (and resultant influence) of Captains, whether on air or sea, as well as their relatively low cost in comparison with the crafts they command, means that even in thirty years' time they are very likely to remain on board and in overall charge of their vessels, though almost exclusively in managerial roles. Exceptions will be for dangerous environments – including military arenas, deep-sea and space – where it may often make far more sense to use highly-sophisticated forms of remote control or fully-autonomous control, for similar reasons as the US military used airborne drones in Afghanistan.

And that brings us to the topic of Cyborgs.

CYBORG VERSUS THE BIONIC WOMAN

Problems in providing senses like Touch (as well as
economic considerations) will postpone the rise of
Bionic Men and Women – although Cyborgs will be
around

FOR USES SUCH as fire-fighting, nuclear work, highly-advanced surgery
and specialized military tasks, either fully self-contained robotic control or
sophisticated 'teleoperator' remote-control will become increasingly
common. But surprisingly to many people, whenever there is any
manipulation of objects involved, it is primarily the *robotic* option that will
be far more common than sophisticated remote-control. The reason is the
human sense of touch: It is immensely sophisticated. With their eyes shut
people can easily distinguish velvet from silk or wet sand from dry. They
can pick up a butterfly or a boulder with the same fingers. The difficulty is
doing the same remotely.

The greatest problem is reproducing sensations on the fingertips and
palms of a distant human operator. Technologists still do not really have
any idea how to do it well other than perhaps direct nerve stimulation
using electronics. However, achieving the resolution of human touch, let
alone being able to stimulate the *correct* pattern of nerves in an operator,
is still a long way off.

ARTIFICIAL HEARING

Although the global number of cochlear implants – all-too-often
dubbed 'bionic-ears' by the press – is rapidly approaching 200,000, the
quality of hearing they offer is still extremely poor in comparison with
normal hearing, primarily because of the challenge of stimulating
auditory nerves in a meaningful way.

46

Enhanced humans

Far easier, in practice, will be for a largely-independent robot to use maybe quite different means of distinguishing things like texture; what a human achieves through touch, a robot might determine by scanning with a laser or exploring with ultrasound. For human operators applying remote control, even using vision to try to compensate for lack of feeling is extremely hard. It is not just absence of a sense of touch that is the problem, but also lack of any sense of where the remote hands actually are (technically known as 'proprioception'). Imagining trying to pick up a butterfly if your whole arm has gone numb, begins to convey the idea.

That is also one of the reasons why bionic limbs for amputees – with advanced engineering taking the place of tissue and bone – will remain far more of a challenge than members of the public expect. It is already possible to build highly-sophisticated prosthetic arms and hands that mechanically operate just like robots, sometimes with even greater freedom of movement than the human joints they replace. It is even possible to tap into signals from existing muscles or nerves to control the position of those prosthetics by thought alone. And, using extra processing power, technologists will become even cleverer with how they do that.

But providing feedback in the form of a sense of proprioception, let alone of touch, is far more difficult. Despite what developers sometimes suggest, for very many decades *no one* is likely to want to amputate an otherwise-healthy hand or arm in order to replace it with an electromechanical replacement. Computerized alternatives may indeed become superior in narrow ways (such as flexibility or sustained grip), but overall they will remain far worse. And for legs it is even more of a challenge because much of walking and running is a form of controlled falling from one leg to the other, so feedback of things like ankle position and muscle tension provides a crucial addition to someone's sense of balance and vision.

As a result, within decades, the most advanced artificial-limbs are set to be far more robotic than many assume, with a large proportion of their control being taken over by on-board computing rather than left to the amputee. Having made the decision to walk in a particular direction, or grasp a particular object, the limbs will very largely take over (to maintain balance or to grip with a light-touch). Just as the journalists of the time are bound to point out, the resulting combination of part-robot and part-human will indeed be a cyborg – a genuine example of the 'cybernetic organisms' beloved of sci-fi. However, to be fair, few people are actually aware of controlling their leg muscles when they walk anyway. The cyborg-approach is not really anything fundamentally new just because the control mechanism happens to reside in silicon rather than the lower-functions of a brain.

In addition, because cyborg development is primarily dependent on increases in computing power rather than on the invention of radically new sensors and feedback mechanisms, it will – at least for a few decades – advance far faster than attempts to build fully-bionic substitutes designed directly to replace the original limbs (in the same way that today someone might change their printer while leaving the rest of their computer system alone). Whatever science-fiction has led people to expect, the reality is that by 2040 the international community will have a small but significant population of Cyborgs, yet very few Bionic Men and Women. And because of the high costs involved, all those cyborgs will have to be rich, or have excellent health-insurance, or be incredibly lucky to have been chosen as human guinea-pigs.

WHY IRON MAN WILL ALWAYS HAVE TO BE SUPERRICH

Sophisticated exoskeletons that enhance healthy people will remain too expensive for all but very-dangerous tasks, and future warfare will not often suit them

MANY FORECASTERS PREDICT that because all this kind of technology will be available within decades, it will inevitably and rapidly also be adopted into specialized environments (if only in the form of exoskeletons that can be fastened around ordinary people) and increasingly factory workers and farmers as well as rank-and-file soldiers will be enhanced into 'superhumans'. In reality, that will not happen. For exactly the same reasons as for amputees, there are tremendous control problems unless almost everything is passed over to computers. Accordingly, to the degree these sorts of enhancements happen at all, it is once again the cyborg-approach that will dominate, not direct control. Even so, take-up will remain low. It is already possible to build a sophisticated exoskeleton to enhance someone's strength and endurance and reduce their vulnerability. Yet even with advancing computer power to compensate for insufficient feedback to the human operator, as with all other robotics it is the *moving parts* that will typically keep exoskeletons prohibitively expensive.

As a result, even in thirty years, the only economically-justifiable applications will be in areas like extreme fire-fighting, highly-dangerous military operations, and work in hazardous commercial environments such as deep-sea or nuclear. Yet for all of these examples, the low volume of production will not only keep prices very high but also mean that reliability will always tend to be an issue; there will never be enough experience built up to iron out every wrinkle of such complex designs. On top of that, the relatively low volumes will not attract major investment unless large manufacturers can justify much of the cost as a form of corporate advertising, or else plan the devices as prototype-applications of

49

technology they can later adapt for higher-volume products. It is little different to the reality behind the largely-handmade supercars of today.

So, even by 2040, there will be far fewer robotic 'enhancements' to humans than the available technology might initially suggest. What is more, the unavoidable calculation that military commanders have to make – deliberately risking the lives of personnel in order to further a mission's objectives – will still result in significant human casualties. This is not so much a consequence of restricted defense budgets or issues of reliability, as of a deep-seated shift toward a fundamentally different form of fighting. Ever since the very-public failure of vastly-superior military strength in Vietnam, guerrilla warfare and in-city paramilitary campaigns have been on the increase. Reinforced by the more recent experiences in Iraq and Afghanistan, that transition will continue.

Despite using exceptionally sophisticated equipment (such as widespread use of increasingly-advanced robotic drones and fully-robotic fighter jets for surveillance or attack, and massively distributed sensors scattered across enemy territory), sophisticated armed-forces will, even more than today, have to interact on foot with 'civilians' – if only to reassure them or try to win them over. Such interaction demands deployment of relatively non-intimidating flesh-and-blood personnel, even though some of the 'noncombatants' they meet may in reality turn out to be hostile. Even if soldiers wear sophisticated body-armor and head-up displays linked to advanced sensing equipment, a Battle for Hearts and Minds tips the balance away from favoring expensive technology – which is the whole reason that insurgents, rebels, freedom-fighters and under-resourced armies will all increasingly choose guerrilla-tactics and terrorism over any form of more-traditional warfare. Even in thirty years' time, politicians will still largely send young men and women – not robots – into battle. Theirs will simply be a different sort of close-combat to that of their predecessors.

THE STRETCHING OF SOCIETY

It is incorrect to predict that as a developed society becomes dominated by Digitization so everything within it will be able to modernize as it does in most sci-fi

INSIDE THE HOME, many of us will increasingly have highly automated devices that will no doubt be called Robots even if some of them are just glorified moving devices without the flexibility or sophistication really to justify the title. And it is Robot Pets that may well be one of the early examples that people are willing to pay significant money for. Although when they are first introduced these pets will be little more than highly-advanced toys with basic simulated emotions, they are likely to have become commonly available fully-fledged virtual companions by 2030, able accurately to read their owner's emotions and respond accordingly. These developments will also tie in with the parallel demand for sophisticated virtual assistants – with the great advantages that unlike traditional pets they will not need to be exercised or toileted and that unlike either pets or human assistants they will potentially be around for as long as their owners will.

More mundane (but still surprisingly sophisticated in terms of processing capability) will be devices like automated vacuum cleaners, lawn mowers, leaf blowers and snow clearers. Each will potentially move from curiosity to practical industrial appliance over the next twenty years. But for most people they will still remain too expensive for the home, and they will be unlikely to become much cheaper over the following decades because their main costs will be mechanical components rather than rapidly-cheapening digital electronics. For similar reasons, despite the amazing videos you may have seen of human-shaped robots that are already able to walk or run or negotiate steep staircases, I can pretty well guarantee that even by 2040 hardly anyone *at all* will have humanoid robots doing the washing, ironing and general cleaning of the house. Sorry.

DIGITIZATION

ASIMO

Probably the most filmed research-robot of the last few years is one called ASIMO that looks like a small white astronaut. It is very impressive. However, what most people do not realize is that there is more than one ASIMO – in reality there are *over a hundred*. What you see on any given video is just a single example from a whole series of progressively advanced models developed by the Honda Motor Company Ltd, which has been heavily researching AI and robotics since 1986.

It will be perfectly possible to make the electromechanical body; we are pretty well there already. And by then there should just about be sufficiently affordable pattern recognition systems and control algorithms to negotiate fully and safely the disorder of the average home (actually, one of the most chaotic environments humans spend time in). But it is the cost of all the complex physical components that will stop the public buying androids. It will simply be a lot cheaper to pay for a person to do the same work. I predict that in 2040 – in hotels, offices and even private homes – this activity will be a whole human profession in its own right. They will call themselves: Cleaners.

There is a really important lesson in that example. Politicians, scientists, Hollywood writers, all tend to assume that as the world economy moves into a computer-dominated age *everything* will progressively get modernized and everybody's lives will change accordingly. But the future will not work that way. The reality of the explosive growth of a High-Tech supertrend superimposed upon everything else in the international community will be that society rapidly becomes stretched.

Those aspects of the past that are deeply reinforced will remain strongly resistant to change, the Legacy Effect in action. Meanwhile, deeply-embedded trends such as Digitization will remain largely unstoppable, another version of the Legacy Effect in action. But the 'unstoppable' High-Tech supertrend is already exploding so fast that there is no time for the 'immovable' aspects of society to adapt. Instead, seismic forces are building, and society risks sheering. It will be as if, overnight,

Polarization

profoundly old-school Victorian politicians found themselves at the height of the Swinging Sixties confronted by a new generation preaching Flower Power. That sort of deep-seated disconnect in society does not resolve quickly. Instead it results in polarization.

Manual factory workers in second-hand robot cars

In just three decades, and even if just driven by the Digitization trend, the future will be a conflict of old and ultra-modern that standard forecasts have not recognized

EVEN AS WE decipher the impact of just a single booster of the High-Tech engine on which we all now depend to sustain the launch trajectory of our global economy, we already reveal a future only three decades away where manual workers still perform mindless tasks in some factories that remain relatively disordered at the same time as office workers engage with sophisticated virtual assistants that extend and amplify their mental capabilities far beyond anything they could achieve alone. Front-line soldiers risk their lives in close combat, yet at home their friends travel in second-hand robotic cars. Rich amputees with replacement limbs, and top-surgeons performing complex (and sometimes remote) operations, increasingly prefer to delegate control to their computers, because it is safer that way.

Through the night, high-speed convoys of driverless trucks head to their destinations where in the early hours low-paid human workers will unload them and begin stacking the supermarket shelves. The food they handle comes from two very-different types of farmers: those who run almost fully-automated arable farms where crops are sown, managed, harvested and stored using advanced robotic tractors, and those who produce livestock in much the same way as their grandparents did. Animal-lovers argue over whether it is preferable to spend the cost of buying a pedigree pet or buying a robotic alternative instead – because apart from ease of looking after, and issues of hygiene and animal rights, the robot pets understand far more of what their owners say, respond to their moods far better, and will never leave them.

Polarization

As a teenage girl walks down a suburban street, a video of the conversation she is having with her friend is automatically recorded three times – by the traffic camera on a nearby lamppost, the security system on the house she is approaching, and the personal video-diary that she herself keeps of every second of her life. And once inside the house, a home-media system not only videos but also transcribes and archives forever her claimed references as she applies for a domestic cleaning job.

That is the reality of what may well be the *least* disruptive thrust generated within the High-Tech engine. All these stresses to society are as nothing compared with the forthcoming rupture in the world economy that is uncovered by decoding the trend detailed in the next chapter. Even today, the strains caused by Digitization are deepening cracks that have already appeared around this second booster to the global economy. In another thirty years, the sudden release of the enormous pressures that will have built are set to split society apart – and forever change what it means to be alive.

CHAPTER SUMMARY
DIGITIZATION

Digitization is on an almost-unstoppable course to a polarized society of virtual-assistants, robot cars, cyborgs and everything on-the-record

Within decades everything will potentially be on-the-record, and personal Virtual Assistants will be needed to access a lifetime's data

- *Accelerating capacities for digital-data storage means it will soon be affordable for members of the general public to record and keep non-stop videos of their lives*
- *Accessing data archives will be so problematic that personal Virtual Assistants will be vital to retrieve the right data and in so doing amplify a person's capabilities*

Digitization of a largely Analog world may be one of the most important transitions for the world economy in five-thousand years

- *Since the 1960s many electronics experts have misinterpreted the systemic reinforcements that long ago turned Moore's Law into a self-fulfilling prophesy*
- *The original reinforcing cycle behind the accuracy of Moore's Law has now turned into something far more relentless that is set to last for several more decades*
- *Computer-chip complexity in fact only indicates the maximum realistic speed at which the far-more-fundamental process of widespread Digitization can accelerate*

Robots will not turn out like in the movies but – especially in the forms of cars and tractors – they will be widespread within decades

- *Many predictions of future applications for robots have deeply underestimated the impact of accounting conventions as well as the costs of mechanical components*
- *Although many expectations for robotics will be dashed, hugely sophisticated yet affordable robotic cars and tractors will be readily available to the public by 2040*

Chapter summary

Many predictions that robotic technology will be used to enhance humans are misdirected – even for some proposed military applications
- *Problems in providing senses like Touch (as well as economic considerations) will postpone the rise of Bionic Men and Women – although Cyborgs will be around*
- *Sophisticated exoskeletons that enhance healthy people will remain too expensive for all but very-dangerous tasks, and future warfare will not often suit them*

The net effect of all the future impacts of Digitization will tend to polarize every aspect of society throughout the international community
- *It is incorrect to predict that as a developed society becomes dominated by Digitization so everything within it will be able to modernize as it does in most sci-fi*
- *In just three decades, and even if just driven by the Digitization trend, the future will be a conflict of old and ultra-modern that standard forecasts have not recognized*

NETWORKING overview

Networking will by 2040 lead to computers capable of human-like interaction and an internet a billion times more powerful than today's

- Top-down Networking will by 2040 result in supercomputers 30,000 times more powerful than today's with human-level machine intelligence

- Bottom-up Networking will by 2040 lead to 'ubiquitous computing' and a 'supernet' a billion times more powerful than today's internet

- Strong AI with the supernet will transform areas like education and health but also bring revolutions in virtual reality and social networking

- Inevitable Networking side-effects will lead to polarized intolerance, loss of privacy and demands for legal Rights of Access to the supernet

- The net effect of Digitization augmented by Networking is a global economy driven by AI and the supernet – and inexplicable without them

SECOND-STAGE BOOSTER

NETWORKING

HOW SUPERCOMPUTERS GET TO BE SO SUPER

Tightly-networked computer processors in the form of supercomputers permit the highest possible overall computing power to be gained from a given level of technology

THE REALLY BIG classic prediction about the future usually goes something like this: *'The power of computers will keep growing exponentially until within only a few decades they will become as sophisticated as the human brain and people will find themselves sharing the planet with Artificial Intelligences that, because their sophistication will continue to grow exponentially, will rapidly overtake the human population in intellect – and from that moment, all bets about the future are off.'* In reality, parts of that prediction are wildly misleading. What we will actually experience will be far more complex. And it will, if anything, be even more counterintuitive.

Contrary to the assumption forecasters usually make, maximum available computing power is not just determined by the exponential growth of processor complexity driven by the Digitization trend covered in the last chapter. Instead, computing capability is increasingly dominated by the second component of the High-Tech supertrend: Networking. Even as recently as twenty-five years ago the developments in linking together different computer processors seemed a very minor trend, but its impact has already arguably overtaken that of Digitization alone. And the main reason is that the influence of Networking operates in *two* directions – it pushes the boundaries of what is possible not only at the top-end of computing but the bottom-end as well.

Starting at the top: Since the first real supercomputers in the 1960s, the technique for achieving otherwise unattainable specs has been to network together cooperating computer processors. That is far more complex than it sounds because everything from cooling the circuits to storing all the data produced is a nightmare. But conceptually, modern supercomputers are nothing more than lots of networked computer chips.

In the past those chips were specially designed, but these days new-generation chips are so expensive to custom-make that supercomputers use networks of mass-produced chips instead, not least because a single one of those chips already has the power of a whole supercomputer a few decades ago. Interestingly, the mass-produced chips already derive some of their increased power by networking together a small number of separate computer-processors (called 'cores') that are all built onto the same chip. The multi-core processor chip in a modern powerful personal computer is, at the microscopic scale, already a networked computer.

BOLDLY GOING WHERE NO MAN HAD GONE BEFORE

The first few decades of early supercomputer development were dominated by the designs of one man – the extraordinarily creative Seymour Cray – initially as part of the Control Data Corporation and then in his own company, Cray Research. I saw my first Cray in the 1980s and was blown away by its ultra-high-tech appearance. My overriding impression was that it *looked* like something from the future. Years later I learned this was in fact completely deliberate – Seymour was a lifelong fan of Star Trek and wanted his supercomputers to look the part.

Today's most powerful supercomputer-design is the 'Sequoia' (tallest tree in the forest). In 2009 the US Department of Energy's National Nuclear Security Administration announced a contract with IBM to design and build a *20-petaflop* supercomputer – that is, capable of 20,000,000,000,000,000 'floating-point operations' per second. To put that in context, those twenty thousand *trillion* calculations a second are equivalent to every human on Earth completing three million computations a second. To achieve that, the Sequoia is designed to network together almost one hundred thousand processors, each with up to sixteen cores. That will result in a network of around 1,600,000 computer cores. This greatest supercomputer to date is scheduled to be fully deployed by the end of 2012.

SELF-LEARNING SOFTWARE

But that kind of networking is just a starting point. It is the already-impressive foundation upon which the explosive growth of top-down networked computing will now build. And to do that, it will probably adopt the same sort of approach as toddlers do. The point is that even those human babies who grow up to be very bright nevertheless are pretty dumb when they are first born. However, they get over that by having an exceptionally sophisticated self-learning program that sucks in everything around them as they try to make sense of the world. Any supercomputer designed to achieve what is known as 'strong' Artificial Intelligence (strong AI) – behavior comparable to human intellect – will have to do the same, or at least inherit such software from an earlier computer.

That is an illustration of the important lesson that AI does not just depend on the power of computer hardware but also on the sophistication of the software that runs on that hardware. And the development of software can lag far behind hardware. Unfortunately, that fact has not stopped some AI researchers in the past getting a little over-passionate.

STRONG A I

Some researchers now use the term 'strong AI' to distinguish it from 'weak AI' (also referred to as 'narrow AI') that does not reach human levels of intelligence. As an alternative to 'strong AI' other experts prefer 'Artificial General Intelligence' (AGI) because that term stresses the breadth of intelligence that humans display.

A small number of well-publicized scientists in the 1970s and 1980s got rather excited by the 'imminent arrival' of Thinking Machines. However, even back then, many of us in the field suspected just how much of a struggle it would be to translate computing power to perceived capability, let alone perceived intelligence. I remember one of the leading AI researchers of the period sharing with me how frustrated he felt that some of his colleagues were playing up the likely speed of development so much. The hype got those researchers funding in the short-term. It created extreme cynicism by the 1990s. As a result, these days most computing-scientists are publically very cautious, despite the private assumption of many of them that they will see AI comparable to their own intelligence within their lifetimes.

What most people do not realize is that self-learning in computers has been around a long time. Indeed, serious work on AI started back in the 1930s thanks to the brilliant work of one of history's greatest unsung heroes: the genius mathematician Alan Turing. Even when he was at university, it was apparent to him that all forms of computer – even the human brain – were conceptually the same, and he had soon proved mathematically that a computer does not have to be limited just to doing arithmetic. That was crucial because he was one of the first advocates of the rule-breaking idea that *everything* in the universe can be represented artificially, even abstract mental states in the human brain. There was no conceptual difference between, say, the biochemical switches (neurons) in the brain and the electrical switches in a calculating machine. This led to the inevitable conclusion that ultimately computers would 'think'.

During World War II, at Bletchley Park in rural England, this extraordinary man was a leading member of the group responsible for deciphering the German 'Enigma' code. Unknown to the outside world, they eventually built the very first electronic computer – but they were bound to secrecy, and for many decades after the war no one learned of their amazing achievement. Alan himself was hounded into suicide at a tragically early age by the official actions of an establishment that disowned him because he was gay. Yet his wonderful legacy lived on, and grew just as he had predicted. By the early 1980s, when I was still a research scientist, it was no longer true that 'a computer can only do what it is programmed to do'. And these days, self-learning algorithms are everywhere. They are how Amazon, for instance, makes such clever recommendations to you that increasingly really are *only* for you. They are how Google so accurately selects sponsored links to add to a search result (which they get paid for if you find any of those sites interesting enough to click on).

These sorts of approaches will keep improving AI. Meanwhile, there are radically-different types of well-funded research that are also improving AI, but are approaching the challenge by analyzing the molecular design of human brains to find out how they work – with the goal of ultimately mimicking the biological design sufficiently well to create working copies. But all this research raises an important question: How will scientists and their governments know if any of these approaches has worked?

SYNTHESIZING A HUMAN BRAIN

The 'Blue Brain Project' running in Lausanne, Switzerland and primarily funded by the Swiss government, was started in 2005 and uses a supercomputer to build progressively advanced models of mammalian brains, with the longer-term goal of simulating the full physiological processes in the human brain – in other words, 'reverse-engineering' a synthetic brain from an original.

PASSING THE TURING TEST

By 2040 supercomputers should be at least 30,000 times more powerful than the best of today and pass the so-called Turing Test for human-level machine intelligence

IN ADDITION TO helping design the world's first electronic computer, and laying down the logical foundation for every type of computer since, Alan Turing also invented what still remains the most practical proposal for dealing with the thorny issue of whether a machine could ever be classed as 'intelligent'. It has become known as the Turing Test and in essence is a form of Blind Date game. He said that if a human-being using, say, a computer terminal can communicate with a hidden something and yet after a reasonable time cannot tell whether that something is human or artificial then for all practical purposes it should be considered as being intelligent – even if in reality it is a *computer*. Anything less (even using apostrophes and calling it 'intelligent') is simply splitting hairs.

It is a deceptively simple test, and more than sixty years after its invention it is still quoted by most computing scientists as the standard against which AI must be measured. Personally, I suspect that when we do want to test a computer for artificial intelligence we will need to add a criterion that the computer actually understands the concepts it is dealing with. After all, we now know that humans can be so gullible that a clever computer-generated imitation (for instance of a famous composer's style of music) can make someone infer far more intelligence than is really being displayed. Also, I am not sure that many of the things most of us say *are* particularly intelligent. So rather than force a candidate computer to make little mistakes because it realizes that 'to err is human', I would rather that it wowed its examiners by demonstrating apparent intelligence without the dumb human bits.

What is more, I do not think that human invigilators should mind very much if the computer can only pass the Turing Test in a relatively narrow field. In practice, it may turn out that to achieve strong AI actually *requires* breadth, we are not sure. But if it does not, then at least initially, it will be impressive enough if an AI system can help come up with new forms of cheap and safe energy, food and water. If it gets confused outside its field of expertise and claims the pop-star Madonna was divine – well, so did lots of her fans. And finally, if a device passes the Turing Test and in the process tells researchers that it is truly conscious and self-aware, then we might as well accept the assertion as fact. After all, that is exactly what everybody does when any human-being makes the same claim, based on far less knowledge of what is really going on inside their head than scientists will know about the AI system.

THE OPPOSITE OF HUMAN

Conceptually, the Turing Test is the exact reverse of the Captcha systems on many current websites that are designed to check if you really are a *human* (and not a computer) by getting you to type in the characters displayed in a deliberately distorted image that is difficult for existing automated pattern-recognition systems to interpret.

The concept of the Turing Test (albeit with slight amendments) is a very powerful one. And from everything I can see, a supercomputer might just pass the Turing Test – at least in a narrow field – as early as 2030. It would be surprising if it was earlier, simply because by then supercomputers are only likely to be about a thousand times more powerful than those of today. But it would be surprising if it was much later than 2040. After all, if Moore's Law consistently slows from doubling every eighteen months (as it maintained for forty years) to doubling every two years (which seems more likely), that would still mean that the supercomputers of 2040 will be about 30,000 times more complex than those of today. As I first published back in the early 1980s, raw computing complexity does not translate into perceived intelligence (it needs the equivalent of a baby's self-learning software to do that), but it is a pretty good indicator of *potential* intelligence. And 30,000 times more complex than today's massively powerful supercomputers – is quite a lot of potential.

MYTH OF THE SINGULARITY

Despite the likelihood of machine intelligence, the concept of a Singularity after which human progress accelerates beyond imagination is based on fundamental errors

IF A SMALL number of extremely expensive supercomputers in 2040 can pass the Turing Test it will be amazingly symbolic but, despite what some cyber-prophets claim, of itself it will not change much day to day. In contrast, what will by then be making a profound difference to civilization will be relatively cheap AI that has *not* passed the Turing Test but that is nevertheless sufficiently advanced to have profound impacts on every aspect of people's lives. For instance, for the first time computers will dramatically change the role of high-end professionals such as doctors, lawyers, scientists and (ironically enough) computer programmers.

What is more intriguing, though, is what will *then* happen. Surely, many suggest, if computer power continues to increase at the same rate, then ten years after a supercomputer has passed the Turing Test and demonstrated an intelligence comparable to that of a human being, it will potentially be thirty times more intelligent. Twenty years after passing the test it will potentially be a thousand times more intelligent.

To be clear: That is not 'potentially as intelligent as a thousand humans' – it is 'potentially a thousand times more intelligent than a single human'. No one can pretend to understand what that means. Consequently, more and more people have begun to use the term 'the Singularity' to refer to that point in the future where synthetic superintelligence drives technical progress so fast that mere mortals will no longer be able to follow it. They often throw in for good measure that this is also the time that people will be able to upload their brains onto silicon to cheat death. And they conclude that the Singularity is therefore the time beyond which it is meaningless to try to forecast the future. Some of the best-informed proponents of this idea calculate the date of the Singularity as being around 2045. I believe they are totally wrong.

NEARING THE ALLEGED 'SINGULARITY'

Vernor Vinge suggested in 1982 that forecasters could not usefully predict the future beyond the time that machine intelligence learned to improve itself and therefore, according to him, exploded into superintelligence. He borrowed the term 'singularity' from theoretical physics to suggest an analogy with the event-horizon of black holes beyond which nothing can be observed.

I have deep respect for their data and their reasoning. But just as with the equally-knowledgeable scientists almost thirty years ago who tried to persuade my editor that Moore's Law could not continue for more than another decade – I think they are nevertheless missing something fundamental.

FLAWS IN THE SINGULARITY

Skipping over concerns about whether Moore's Law can be expected to hold far into the second half of the century (as already stated, it *will* eventually break down, and even superintelligences are not immune to the laws of physics), the real problem with the idea of the Singularity is *people*. In all my analyses of how society really operates, I see no evidence at all that escalating AI – even if it is possible over several decades – will in practice result in a Singularity. On the contrary.

Firstly, leaders do not tend to give up authority to more intelligent candidates. Instead they use them to help consolidate their authority, just as in literature King Arthur used the far more powerful and intelligent Merlin. CEOs occasionally have genius-level IQs, but it is rare. Likewise, top politicians and statesmen are universally street-smart and often have great interpersonal skills (at least when it suits them). But they do not necessarily have exceptional intelligence. So it will remain. Presidents and Prime Ministers and all their top politicians may become increasingly dependent upon the advice of machines – just as, out of sight of the public, they today depend on personal advisors and some incredibly bright people in their civil services – but they will not be inclined to let machines replace them.

Nor will the machines have unlimited control over the finances and other resources needed to create their next generation, any more than individual government or corporate department-heads have today. Nor will it be any easier for intelligent machines with different backgrounds to work together than it is for genius-level humans. Imagine, for instance, linking together superintelligent computers originally developed by the US Department of Defense, the Chinese-Communist Party, the Vatican and Google. Put another way, it will not be easy at all. In addition, the machines are unlikely even to have the same level of IQ, so that will not help either, even if they want to work together or can be encouraged to work together by their closest human colleagues – which for reasons of local vested interest they often will not.

But there is a further, even more powerful reason why the Singularity will not happen in the way that many futurologists suggest. Even if machines *are* put in charge because humans feel comfortable that the machines will remain 'friendly' (with each other as well as humans), and despite very different mind-sets the machines can nevertheless cooperate, and with their superintelligence they can devise solutions to world problems – *they have still got to manage what by then will be the best part of ten billion humans.* And human society is full of Legacy Effects than cannot simply be changed overnight (as Greek politicians found with the Eurozone crisis).

Profound Legacy Effects mean that overall change is massively slowed down. And some bits alter, others do not, things get out of alignment, that creates unintended side-effects, those must be addressed in their own right, but then the original momentum for change is lost. In other words, even if the Singularity ever started, it would rapidly get bogged down and stall. Even if superintelligent machines were granted the absolute optimal starting conditions (which is highly unlikely) they would find it no easier to manage ten billion humans than today's statesmen would if all their citizens were toddlers.

PROBLEMS WITH UPLOADING CONSCIOUSNESS

And finally, just to lay the idea to rest, despite what a few eminent scientists have suggested to the press, I am afraid that people will *never* be able to 'upload their brain' onto a computer as a way of escaping the decay of their biological original. There are theoretical ways humans could achieve relative immortality by other means, but that is not one of them.

NETWORKING

It does appear to be true that rigorously copying a living brain in sufficient detail will indeed accurately replicate not just memories but also consciousness and self-awareness as well (which seem to be properties that automatically emerge from the complex interactions of a sufficient number of appropriately interconnected neurons). But that is the problem – the process *replicates* consciousness, it does not *move* it. Uploading your brain will create a clone that shares with you all the same memories up to that point. But the original 'you' will still be 'you' trapped in biological tissue. And if the process of uploading your brain actually destroys your biological brain in the process, then you will die – even though the 'clone-you' will feel like you successfully transported.

Conceptually it might be possible to supplement neurons with bionic equivalents (or even, somehow, remote computer-based neurons) that, for example, throughout a considerable period gradually 'took-over' from dying cells in the brain. That would allow a continuity of self-awareness. But it is a fundamentally different approach to the idea of rapidly 'uploading' someone's brain in one go.

Even as a kid watching Star Trek (and learning that the Transporter on board the Enterprise scanned someone's molecules as it dematerialized them, sent that information to another location, and then built up the same pattern of molecules at a remote location) I soon worked out that every time Captain Kirk beamed to the planet surface he was actually being killed and a few seconds later an identical actor picked up the dialogue. Spock never seemed bothered, but I was. And for a simple reason. If the transporter did *not* simultaneously dematerialize the molecules it scanned, the TV-series would end up with an escalating number of Kirks; so poor William Shatner was obviously being bumped off each time he passed through the Transporter.

THE AI ARMS-RACE

The strategic advantages of access to human-level AI will lead to a form of arms-race not only amongst Defense Departments but potentially also well-funded religions

FUTUROLOGISTS DO NOT tend to mention the following: One of the more telling indicators of the next thirty years will be if any of the general public even gets to hear that the first supercomputer has been certified as intelligent. After all, it took about forty years for the Official Secrets Act to release the information that during World War II Alan Turing and others had built the very first electronic computer 'Colossus' in England, before anyone else.

It is largely unclassified that, quite understandably, for several decades important AI research has been funded around the world by many military and security services. But the later stages of such research will necessarily be highly classified. That is partly because no country will want to lose any potential strategic advantage, and partly because the work becomes rather sensitive in a very different way. Those officials that I have spoken to who are responsible for such funding do not seem particularly bothered by the concept of eventually letting computers make lethal decisions, even on a major scale. Conceptually I agree with them, because under stress-conditions it is almost impossible for even the best-trained humans to adhere to the large number of engagement directives they are expected to follow, let alone accurately choose the best strategy to protect the maximum number of lives overall.

But deciding to give computers that sort of power is a deeply political issue, not a technical or logical one. For that reason, humans will very likely be kept in the loop although ideally (at least from the perspective of those in charge) the press – and so the general public – will be kept out of it. Hence, the highly-classified nature of any such work. Anyway, for reasons of national security, full disclosure of the most impressive advances is unlikely to make much sense. The same, of course, is true with other government uses of AI. Not least in Intelligence – there is a clue to AI's relevance in the name. The current reality is that amongst the major political powers, nuclear proliferation is something to worry about in emerging nations, but is not what the heavy-hitters themselves are striving for. AI is becoming what the new, far-more-covert 'arms race' is all about. It has already started. And over the next two decades, as political leaders are increasingly advised that rival economic or military powers are making major investments in machine intelligence, and achieving major breakthroughs, expect the AI arms-race to hot up.

Much more surprising to most people is that, from what I can determine, some of the major religions will not want to be left out of the AI arms-race either. They will start late, but within the next two decades it will dawn on a number of religious leaders that maybe they *do* conceptually have an idea of what it means to interact with an intelligence a thousand times, a million times, a billion times more powerful than themselves. And, as leaders of organized religions across millennia have realized, they will also appreciate that knowledge is influence – if not actual power.

The largest organized religions have got very deep pockets, with Roman Catholicism and Islam by far the richest in terms of global assets and annual income (with the Vatican way ahead in terms of centralized control). But as might be expected, the entry into the race of some of the Faiths is likely to spur on some of the State powers. Not least because some of the Faiths effectively *are* State powers in some parts of the world.

YOUR TRUSTED BEST (ARTIFICIAL) FRIEND

Corporations developing AI will focus on extremely-fast human-level intelligence that is easy to interact with rather than vastly-superior levels of machine intelligence

NONE OF THE developments yet considered even takes account of the immensely powerful corporate entries into the race that, promoted with huge marketing budgets, will be sponsored by venture capitalists increasingly desperate to profit from AI-related stock. Like the dot.com bubble of the '90s, by 2030 the global economy will see fortunes being thrown at anything with AI mentioned in its prospectus. But once a computing system wins the final 'Loebner prize' (by passing the most difficult version of the Turing Test), I think that the most likely direction that commercial development will take is toward 'intelligence amplifiers' for humans, rather than stand-alone devices. Apart from anything, this will naturally follow on from the virtual assistants that many people will already use to manage their huge personal archives of data and to access what is public of everyone else's.

At a bare minimum, it will be like having a trusted and very bright friend always at hand – a Jeeves to a Bertie Wooster, if you like. Far more likely is that, building on techniques developed for computer-game consoles, great strides will be made in how intuitively to interact with personalized AI systems so that it is in fact far faster and more effective than communicating with a human friend would be. And while on the topic of interacting with AI systems, let me highlight that – despite its near-universal acceptance – I am not convinced by the logic in the other part of the Singularity argument that assumes that a hundred times the computing power of the first machines that pass the Turing Test will result in machine-intelligence a hundred times greater than a human being (and therefore something that people cannot even imagine).

NETWORKING

LOEBNER PRIZE

Since 1990 the Loebner Prize (named after Hugh Loebner, the original sponsor) has been awarded each year to the AI system that judges consider most human-like. The format is that of the Turing Test. There are two additional one-time prizes that are yet to be claimed: the first computer that judges cannot distinguish from a human using only text, and the first that is indistinguishable using text, vision and sound. When a computer claims this last prize, the competition will end. I suspect that – if only because it will have been around for so long – it is the Loebner Prize that symbolically will be taken as the indicator that for the first time Homo sapiens is sharing the planet with a non-human intelligence of comparable sophistication.

I think it is far more likely that many of the designs will still only result in broadly human-levels of IQ – but will *run a hundred times faster.* That is actually extremely easy to imagine. It is almost certainly far cheaper and more reliable to build (because conceptually it keeps the same high-level design but runs it on ever-faster hardware). And it is also very much easier to interact with. Moreover, people should not get carried away with the idea that using 'intelligence amplifiers' is a fundamentally new concept. It is not. It is similar to what leaders have done for at least five-thousand years – surrounding themselves with others who make them far stronger and smarter than they would be alone. That is what start-up companies are. And the most successful start-ups eventually turn into immensely powerful and sophisticated multinationals that are around at the same time as small and medium-sized businesses as well as 'unamplified' individuals. They all co-exist. That is a far closer analogy to how humanity is likely to ensure that it *leverages* superintelligence, rather than 'standing aside and deferring to its betters' as those believing in the Singularity claim will happen.

As already suggested on page 54, passing the Turing Test will at least initially split the international community into two very bright but different 'species' of biological intelligence and machine intelligence, though there is no fundamental reason why these two species cannot rapidly merge. Either way, the advent of human-level AI will, as I also said,

Top-down

change people's whole concept of what it means to be 'alive'. Yet in many ways, even the very real prospect of human-level AI within decades is just the tip of an iceberg. Deeply symbolic as such occurrences will be, their impact alone will be relatively minor in comparison with what will be going on at the same time. The reason I say that is that I have so far only revealed the *top-down* impact of Networking combined with Digitization. Everything considered in this book up to now – artificial intelligence, recording every aspect of someone's life, robot cars and so on – is as nothing in comparison with what will *actually* happen. Up until this point, I have been rather underplaying the full power of Digitization augmented by Networking.

Ubiquitous Computing in Everything You Own

The concept of individual personal-computers will be replaced by so-called 'ubiquitous computing' in which almost every object contains an on-line processor

SO FAR IN this book I have tended to use the term 'computer'. That gives the impression that the concept of the personal computer or laptop or stand-alone mobile phone will survive. None of them will. In fact, I suspect that within this current decade everyone around the world will have completely stopped using the term 'mobile phone' and will simply refer instead to a 'mobile' – because even the cheapest will contain sufficient accelerometers, lenses, GPS trackers and other devices that its telephoning ability will no longer dominate its wide range of on-the-move benefits.

What happens to the mobile will happen to everything. The cost of basic computing and sensors will become so incredibly cheap that it will be put into almost anything. It is important to realize that the Lunar Excursion Module landed on the moon using less computer power than is in modern-day calculators that are given away for free. Amazingly, the computer power in some of today's mobile phones is greater than the best mainframe computer I had access to at university – which was one of the best commercially-available machines in the world. Over the next few decades the general public across nearly all of the international community will see an explosion of 'computing' devices. Each of them will be Internet-Enabled. And *that* is how the bottom-up impact of Networking will come into play.

Almost every computing device will potentially be able to interact with all the others using the equivalent of a 'Facebook for devices'. One implication is that a single remote control – it could well be a person's all-powerful Mobile – will potentially be able to drive everything its owner interacts with. There will initially be battles over which industry-standards vendors follow, not least for things like the profile-data used in social networking, but increasingly users will be unaware of all those sorts of details. Most of the growing complexity will be hidden, just as happened in the 1990s as the average user became blissfully unaware of the computer languages in which their application-software was written. Website addresses and URLs will largely disappear from view. And the opportunities that come from far greater bandwidth on both landlines and wireless connection will mean that the Networking trend transforms everything.

Imagine that nearly all items you own, including everything from clothing and food packaging to kitchen appliances and TVs, not only all have their own miniature computers and sensors but (via a wireless network) those computers can all talk with each other and (via wired networks) they can also talk to all the huge number of distributed computers throughout your home and your office and throughout all the towns and cities that you visit. And via the internet all those computers can in turn interact with their counterparts across the whole of the global economy stretched around the planet. And all those can access any and all knowledge that is publically available. And, because of incredibly low memory costs, that knowledge is increasingly representative of pretty well everything that is going on around the world. Welcome to the 'Supernet'.

Computers will disappear. Just like mains electricity, computing power will simply be there. As a result, the impact of such so-called 'ubiquitous computing' when combined with the Networking trend will be astonishing. Moreover, because the precursor to the internet was fortunately originally designed so that the network would keep going even if individual nodes were physically destroyed, the supernet will be inherently resilient. Although any computer network is potentially vulnerable to cyber-attacks such as hacking, computer viruses or attempts to overload selected servers (bright college students as well as cyber-terrorists and a few rogue states are already deeply experienced in all this), the supernet's extraordinary diversity will keep it fundamentally robust.

WELCOME TO THE SUPERNET

Today's internet will continue to explode in terms of numbers of discrete devices and the increasing sophistication of those devices all linked in increasingly useful ways

THE SUPERNET WILL not just be robust, but also extremely powerful. The reason is that the growth rate of the internet is driven by a lot more than just Moore's Law. Back in the 1970s I was lucky enough to get a chance to operate the original ARPANET two decades before it exploded as the internet. It was fun, and even back then it seemed obvious that the idea had potential. But there was not, frankly, a lot you could do with it – other than type messages to fellow-geeks in a few computer-labs on other continents. After all, there were relatively few computers in the world, and only a very small proportion of those were connected to ARPANET.

But that is the point. The more computers that connect to a network the more valuable it becomes. It is like the early days of the telephone system. If there were only two telephony pioneers connected, that was nice but they could only ever talk with each other. If there were three people connected, however, they could be configured for three quite distinct conversations. Four telephones could be connected in *six* different ways. Five could have *ten* different connections. A hundred could make almost *five-thousand* different connections. Today, a million subscribers can in total make just under *half a trillion* different connections. That is more connections than there are stars in the whole of the Milky Way. And there are already several *hundreds of millions of subscribers* to the internet.

But that is only the beginning. Even if only the same number of people each day joined the internet (in other words the growth was linear), then as just shown the usefulness of the internet would nevertheless be accelerating. However, the number of computers connecting to the internet actually appears to be growing exponentially. So there are two forms of acceleration on top of each other. Now add to that the fact that, thanks to Moore's Law, the complexity of each of those computers is on

78

average also increasing exponentially. The combination is astounding. The power of today's internet is the product of three kinds of acceleration all superimposed on top of each other: exponential numbers of distributed computing devices of exponentially growing average complexity all linked all of the time via astronomically increasing interconnections on the supernet. If it is reasonable to call the growth based on Moore's Law alone an 'explosion' then, in fairness, the mounting power of the internet is closer to TNT triggering the nuclear-fission detonator of a hydrogen-fusion bomb. By 2040 the supernet will be approaching a billion times more powerful than today's internet.

POWER OF THE SUPERNET

A very rough indicator of the 'power' of the supernet in 2040 corresponds to a continuation of Moore's Law at Intel's current commitment of doubling every two years, which results in about 30,000 times the processing capability of today's chips. So far the number of websites seems to have grown exponentially since the mid-1990s. Even at current rates it would be fifty times larger by 2040. But that heavily underestimates the number of connected computers in thirty years once you factor in that people who have one PC today are likely to own *hundreds* of web-enabled devices by then – many of them throw-away – and each linked onto the internet. Under those circumstances, even the equivalent of two hundred times the number of 'average computers' connected to today's internet is still probably a conservative estimate for growth over three decades. 'Metcalfe's Law' states that the value of a network is proportional to the square of the number of nodes – giving an 'increase in connectedness' of 40,000 times that of today's internet. So in total that is 40,000 times more interconnections to a range of devices that on average are 30,000 times the processing capability. That is already 1.2-billion times the power of today's internet. The point is that, larger or smaller, the real figure will be *extremely* large.

Education and Healthcare once the Supernet gets going

Education goals will utterly change once most information is instantly available – and healthcare will likewise be transformed by on-line diagnosis and telemedicine

TURBOCHARGED BY INCREASING levels of machine intelligence, the supernet will offer inconceivable access to new ideas as well as archives of old ideas. It will permit almost anybody to access that knowledge and create something new as a result. Even today, roughly a quarter of the world's population has online access (resulting in extraordinary opportunities even in poor rural areas), and open-review experiments like Wikipedia are exploring how truth, knowledge and accuracy can often emerge from decentralized sources in a way that has never been possible before.

TRULY-REMOTE ACCESS

Even using mobile phones in their basic form, creative people employ them for much more than just telephony and texting. In Kenya, for example, the semi-nomadic Maasai people transfer phone-credit by text message and so use the phone network as a mini-bank. And some of today's impacts of the internet on otherwise isolated communities are already both staggering and inspiring. For instance, remote Ethiopian farmers wishing to sell their coffee beans can use a coffee-exchange that within seconds gives them access to the world market.

Indeed, there is a good chance that one of the first publically acknowledged AI systems to pass the Turing Test will have grown up on the supernet just as a baby explores its world at home, possibly with lots of 'amateur' help similar to the input that keeps Wikipedia evolving. It may even have leapfrogged the funding that otherwise would be needed, as a result of members of the public volunteering otherwise unused computing capacity using what is already a well-established technique known as 'grid computing'.

ON THE GRID

One of the most successful examples of Grid Computing is the 'SETI@home' system that uses the downtime of home-computers to analyse radio-telescope data for signs of extra-terrestrial intelligence. At any one time the resultant grid-computer comprises a network of hundreds of thousands of small computers worldwide – providing SETI with an overall processing power comparable to that of a supercomputer.

In principle all of this offers the potential for seismic shifts in education. However, from all my analyses, I expect formal education to be painfully slow in adapting. The old ways are *very* deeply entrenched. The real issue here will have little to do with *how* educators should use the supernet to support education. It will have everything to do with *what* as human beings it makes sense to learn when nearly all codified knowledge is instantly available, languages can be translated in real-time, and computers can solve extremely complex problems. It is very much easier to teach facts, techniques and solutions than creativity, judgment and problem-solving.

Furthermore, already today there are growing concerns that children who have never known life without the internet are finding it harder to work through a long-form book (whether on-screen or in a physical form) than to surf the loosely-associated collection of short-form abstracts that is largely what web sites are. If that is true, then it is a problem because they are two very different forms of learning. And one form cannot substitute for the other. Reading a summary of ten brilliant novels is not the same as reading one of them in full. Learning a lot about a wide range of physics is not the same as mastering sufficient details of quantum mechanics as to be able to make a breakthrough.

Just as the supernet has the potential, however slowly, to overhaul Education, the same is true of the Health Services. Even today, it has become common practice for patients to check out the internet before and after visiting their doctor. Increasingly members of the public will find even the most reputable medical sites offering expert-system pre-diagnosis. Within twenty years, telemedicine will be common – especially given that a surprising number of medical examinations do not require a sense of touch or smell, and by that time high-definition video and sound will be taken for granted. For much the same reasons, remote nursing (or at least monitoring) will also be possible. And it is not just interactions with doctors and nurses that will rapidly evolve.

Virtual Reality systems will be *really* good by 2040. There is a deeply established trend from the computer-game industry pushing far into the future that almost guarantees there will be some form of headset available that is made in sufficient numbers to provide, at a bare minimum, affordable computer-generated 360° sound along with 3-D vision of a resolution pretty well indistinguishable from being in the real world. You can make up the rest: Start with the recognition that so many technology developers are deeply influenced by blockbuster Sci-Fi movies, then just throw in a dose of *The Matrix* combined with a helping of *Avatar* – and what have you got?

WHY ARTIFICIAL REALITY WILL BECOME SO ADDICTIVE

Readily-affordable Virtual Reality systems will be addictive as computer-generated environments and even relationships become superior to those offered in the real-world

EVEN WITHIN ANOTHER decade, the consumer computing power needed for real-time simulation of a completely artificial world will not be a problem. And that opens up amazing options for interacting with the supernet. Why should people look at a 2-D screen instead of looking around a 3-D object? Why should someone interact with someone else via a screen, when both could step into a virtual computer-generated world and interact 'in person'? And when interacting with other people in cyberspace – or at least interacting with the 'avatar' they have chosen to represent their appearance – then why should people feel forced by convention to look as they do in real life when they can instead be whatever look, age, gender or indeed species that they choose?

Already today, when tens of millions of people interact daily in virtual environments ranging from *World of Warcraft* and *Habbo Hotel* to *IMVU* and *Second Life*, those who are able to choose what their avatar looks like often select a form that is different from their real-world appearance. Or at least I assume they are different, given that on the average High Street there are not as many well-toned passers-by wearing skin-tight leotards. On the supernet, factors such as hair colour and number of wrinkles and skin-color and gender are increasingly likely to be a matter of choice – and those selections will not be fixed for life. They will not even be fixed for a day. Imagine the freedom of virtual reality in 2040: When the physical world can be grey and small and petty there are other worlds beckoning. And in many ways that cyber universe is just as real as the physical world, because it is possible to run a business there, earn a salary there, make friends there. What is really interesting is that the 'products' that people can buy in a virtual world – say a new sofa for their avatar to recline on in cyberspace – can also be something that if they find they like the look of it they can have delivered to their home *in the real world.*

But then again, if the product is *only* virtual (maybe a beautiful garden to walk through, or an exotic bird to visit an existing virtual garden, or a new face) then it can potentially be designed and sold by almost anybody. Those 'manufacturers' will not need a factory, just their computing terminals. Virtual products can be generated by the many, not just the few. That has major implications for economics. And it is already a nightmare being considered by tax authorities. After all, if a product is made and sold in cyberspace by multiple people in different countries using a distributed computer grid, then which nations get to tax which transactions?

ESCAPING THE REAL WORLD

Many serious discussions about the future of the internet seem to dwell on its serious uses. But that really does not accurately reflect human nature. Non-serious uses will be huge. In addition to the obvious uptake for pornography (which for more than a century has driven the adoption of numerous new-media), imagine being able to walk around a Google Earth that is an accurate representation of the real original. Then combine that idea with the fact that some of the virtual products available to buy may be whole virtual worlds in their own right. This begins to hint at how explosive – but also completely unpredictable – the *details* of this part of the future are. You can potentially do so much of what you can in the real world. But the difference is that you can also fly. You can move around surrounded by utter beauty. You can create fantastical environments. You can be whatever you want to be. And no one can ever physically make you do anything again.

Of course you will still need to eat and go to the bathroom. That is a bit of catch. And there is something wonderful about smelling fresh air, feeling the sun on your skin, and touching something and knowing it is *real* (or at least 'a more consistent illusion' depending on your philosophical point of view). But it is easy to begin to see why the alternative of watching a TV documentary, even in high-definition 3-D with full surround sound, may begin to seem a little tame. In due course it may be possible, just as in *The Matrix* and *Avatar*, to kid senses into smelling 'fresh air' and feeling the 'sun' and touching something 'real' even though you are actually in cyberspace. But, for the same reasons as explained on page 46 with regard to bionic limbs, that sort of tie-in to the human nervous system is such a challenge (and is so relatively underfunded) that it is very unlikely to be commercially available by 2040 even if there were a fundamental breakthrough – which would most likely come from a computer-games manufacturer.

For some, living much of the time in virtual reality is a really exciting thought. For others it is scary. But whichever emotion you feel, as increasingly sophisticated AI systems become available – time-shared across multiple users because, as this is virtual reality, you do not need access while you are asleep – you will not always need even to interact with other humans. You can have a glorious and meaningful relationship with a computer-generated entity who (forget about physical security) will not *mentally* hurt you either.

This initially all feels like a bit of a slippery slope. But I find it extremely hard to come up with a convincing scenario as to why, once the technology is there, it will not happen. This is not one of those things like the video phone that, although readily available via Skype, the general public still has not fully latched onto. Quite to the contrary. When I analyze what drives most individuals it all becomes rather likely that some will substantially prefer virtual reality to real reality. When you add in today's official concerns about existing widespread 'internet addiction' in South Korea (the most wired society on the planet), the likelihood that a vastly more alluring supernet will be even more addictive seems almost certain. In which case, governments had better work out how best to manage the situation – far in advance.

SOCIAL NETWORKING
IN A CYBER-SOCIETY

Social networking systems will become immensely sophisticated as profile data is continuously mined and made available in real-time during real-world interactions

EVEN WITH EVERYTHING I have already covered about how the exponential Networking trend will interact with Digitization, I still have not focused on one final but crucial aspect: Social Networking. The recent explosion of services like Twitter and Facebook are a very small symptom of what is actually building. One way or another, the supernet will need to know where everybody is and what most of their associated devices are doing. There is nothing inherently surprising or sinister about that. But it opens up extraordinary opportunities that many companies are already very eager to exploit.

For a start it allows really sophisticated versions of social networking services that, for example, inform a user when they are near someone subscribing to the service who has a specified profile – whether that is 'a stranger who knows a friend of mine' or 'someone who has got a job vacancy for someone with my profile' or 'someone with a profile I like that is looking for a one-night relationship with someone like me'. Combine that with a form of Augmented Reality (for instance, the screen on your mobile superimposing information on top of the image of the real-world you are pointing it at) and you can scan the street that your mobile has guided you to and see the names of every registered occupant for each house in front of you, along with all those people's contact data. That is no more information than can be found in today's phone books, just a lot more convenient.

But if such information is combined with the picture, age and detailed profile of each individual living in the street, then it starts to seem invasive – even though that is only a combination of a the data in a telephone directory and the publically available profile-data millions have already posted on today's internet. Now imagine that you use the Augmented Reality option on your mobile when you are at an office party, or shopping, or at an exhibition, or a concert – and your mobile gives you the name, contact details and profile of everyone around you. All of this has wide-ranging implications. Many potential concerns are already being talked about. But there are also some less-obvious backlashes...

LINKING YOUR WAY TO POLARIZED INTOLERANCE

The supernet will polarize intolerance as those holding unrepresentative views are nevertheless able to avoid much exposure to ideas other than those similar to their own

AS THINGS STAND, the social-networking developments of the kind just described seem inevitable. But there will be many unexpected consequences. There is the obvious side-effect that the concept of 'friendship' can become devalued by including many people who are actually just 'acquaintances' or even just 'contacts'. Early analysis of social networking sites suggests that, just as in the physical world, those who claim a hundred or more 'friends' actually only have a handful of relationships with whom they truly have close interaction, and the others in their network largely behave like voyeurs.

What is more, living in a fishbowl (whether it is a rural village or a cyberspace community) can encourage the habit of someone seeking validation from the group for everything they do. They only really feel happy by telling the group that they are happy; making a decision involves first telling the group the decision they are planning to make. But in cyberspace, this very-human social interaction can become rather warped because there is often a distorted sense of reality with no real consequences. After all, unlike in a rural village, it is very easy for an individual to drop some cyberspace acquaintances if they do not like what the person has done. And killing someone in a virtual-reality game has very different consequence to those of the real world.

There is a far more important unreality to cyberspace. The supernet will, just like today's internet, cater to a diversity of taste (in everything from music and literature to dating and pornography) that previously could never practically have been supported. In general that is a good thing. But combined with increasingly high communication bandwidths

Side-effects

and sophisticated virtual reality, it will have some very deep social implications.

That is because there is an alluring quality to narrowcasting – where a message or film or bulletin is not broadcast to all the 'average people' but is narrowly focused only on a small clique who are all just like each other. Even today, if someone only reads blogs and visits sites that are written by people who think as they do, it is remarkably easy for them to fall into the trap of believing that those ideas are representative of a broader population. Or at least they draw undue comfort that it is *their* views that are patently correct. Organized religions have demonstrated the tremendous strength of this sociological phenomenon for millennia. More recently, political activists have done the same.

However, up until now, unless locked away in a cloister or a stately home it was hard to avoid frequent interaction with those who held different views. And often, if only because of the need to work with those people, such interaction bred a form of cautious acceptance of diversity. As far as I can tell, historically that sort of 'forced tolerance' has been no bad thing. And certainly, cities have typically been far more tolerant places to live than villages. But as large numbers all disappear into virtual cyber-villages populated by like-minded individuals, those days may fast be disappearing. That is a potential worry. If the phenomenon is deliberately manipulated in the pursuit of extremes in Faith or Politics then it becomes a significant concern. The polarization that would follow would at best run counter to what is needed for a Global Renaissance. At worst, it would totally undermine it.

THE ABDICATION OF PRIVACY AND GOING VENETIAN

Personal privacy will become far less about civil-liberties and much more about perceived fairness for supernet-users trading their privacy for free-access to providers

MOST PEOPLE THINK that concern about personal privacy in the future is a civil-liberties issue – in other words that the main risks are an erosion of the rights that protect individuals from the State. After all, the world changed so much after the 9-11 attacks on the Twin Towers that it is perfectly reasonable to question if governments are slipping into a Surveillance Society. It is not just that now we all take for granted enhanced passport checks and airport security. But most people tacitly acknowledge that their mobile-phone company tracks their location all the time their phone is turned on, their credit card company does the same each time they pay a bill, and every website they access and email is recordable by their internet service provider. Our cars' locations are registered and recorded by the myriad police cameras on the roads that automatically read every license plate. If we use an electronic season-ticket or take money from an ATM, that is registered too. And we are each routinely recorded on video surveillance almost anywhere we walk in a modern city.

In addition, the Security Services can, if appropriate, gain access to all this data about us. And anyway, in many countries – for instance across the European Union – it is already legal for the police to hack into a citizen's personal computer to conduct 'remote searching' of their hard-drive without a warrant. All these examples are *why* most people think that concern about personal privacy in the future is a civil-liberties issue. But they are wrong. Future privacy is primarily going to be a commercial issue. And the way that 'privacy issues' will be resolved is already pretty clear – all because of what happened throughout the last decade.

Side-effects

Ten years ago, cyberspace was something of a virtual car-boot sale. It was a flea market of everything from free information to real products, all jumbled together with no one in overall charge. But like any market, however loud a stall-owner shouted, most people did not find their way to that site because there was so much else to see, and every other site owner was trying their best to grab attention. Seeing all the confusion, a few people (such as Google, Yahoo!, MSN and AOL) stood at the entrance to the market offering free directions. The most successful made good money by including paid advertising that was customized to what we were each searching for. As the alternative was that we would have to pay just to enter the market, everyone was happy – free entrance and free directions not just to what we originally wanted but also to other sites that looked interesting. What was not to like? And that is how it all started.

Today, the global economy pays for the 'free' power of the internet by its users sharing information about who we are, what we like, and how we spend our money. If we use a free email service then the content of our messages is scanned to look for key phrases that suggest the types of advertising to display next to our emails. We visit a site and it places small software 'cookies' on our computer that recognize us in the future, just as a shopkeeper might, and keeps track of which parts of the site we visit. We join a Loyalty Scheme (whether for an airline, a supermarket or a hotel chain) and each time we register a purchase so we add to the years-old profile the company is building of our lifestyle, preferences and purchasing patterns. We buy or sell items online using a 'secure' service, and the patterns not just of our purchases but of everyone else's are mined for information that may prove valuable.

And none of this even touches on the information traded on social networking sites where the minutiae of people's lives are displayed on public view in return for free access to the service – despite the fact that an embarrassing video on Facebook or YouTube, or an indiscretion on Twitter, may remain to haunt someone for the rest of their lives, in every job-interview, at the start of each relationship. And in police-states, activists risk torture to make them disclose their social-networking passwords so as to reveal who their acquaintances are.

Of course, it is very easy on-line for people to lie about their profile. Or have multiple profiles. And I expect that for many people that will become their Defense of Choice as they welcome the supernet into their lives. The closest historical equivalent is the original *Carnevale di Venezia* during which, long before today's tourist pretense, for several months of the year the residents of Venice all wore masks and costumes to hide their identity. It was the solution that the Venetians came up with to survive in their own claustrophobic fishbowl. I strongly suspect that within a few decades, whether as a reassurance in the augmented reality of the real world or as a lifestyle choice in the virtual reality of cyberspace, many people will choose to 'go Venetian'.

HOW TO TRADE FREEDOM FOR FREE-ENTRY

As the supernet becomes increasingly crucial, the international community will demand that the rights of service-providers are curtailed to protect Rights of Access

THE UNCONTROLLED EMERGENCE of the supernet is now practically unstoppable, not least because the original spirit of the founders of the internet was to resist authority and encourage openness. The British computer-scientist credited with inventing the World Wide Web, Sir Tim Berners-Lee, encoded 'free access' into the internet by ensuring that the structure of the web was inherently non-hierarchical. That ethic is so deeply embedded into how the system works that most people just take it for granted. And on top of all that, the internet resists censorship because it is designed to work around any zones that are not operating correctly. When the Iranian authorities try to block Twitter traffic about social unrest, or the Chinese government attempts to censor some websites while maintaining the economic and social benefits of access to others, it is technologically very difficult to do.

The same is true of preventing illegal downloading. Those who have never known anything different increasingly take such free-access as a right, and will happily download copyrighted music and the latest film releases even though they would never consider stealing in any other form. This has already broken the business-model of the music industry. It is set to do the same not just to Hollywood but to software-providers generally. Blocking-tactics like the short-term stop-gap of 3-D cinema releases will not stem the tide, especially as 3-D TV becomes well-established over the next ten years. In a similar way, within a decade or so there will be a series of important battles to decide how the physical owners of the computer systems running virtual worlds can retaliate. These skirmishes will often be seen as the law catching up with technology. But they will be rebellion.

SMUGGLING PAST WEB CENSORS

If an advanced government monitors all internet traffic within its borders in order to prevent its citizens from accessing 'subversive' websites, how can such sophisticated censorship be overcome? Prototype software called Telex solves the problem by allowing users to hide an invisible data-tag within an apparently innocent visit to an uncensored site. That encrypted and disguised tag can only be read by an internet router outside the country, which then redirects the user to the desired banned site and cleverly disguises the data sent back from that website (to make it look like innocent data from what is considered to be a safe site) as it is smuggled back past the government's cyber-censor.

The deeply fundamental question being fought over will in fact be whether system-owners, or even governments, are allowed to *intervene* like Ancient Greek gods into virtual reality. Can they get away with deleting someone from their system if that person does not behave as they want? Or do the owners of the host computer and the original designers of the social network or virtual world not actually have *any* such rights? After all, just because someone owns something or created it does not always mean they can do whatever they like to it. Someone can breed a pet, but they are not usually allowed to torture it. Ultimately, given the foundation that has already been laid, it is the 'freedom fighters' on the internet that are set to win that round. So the game will then change. Massively sophisticated social-networking systems will lure the general public into greater and greater disclosure. And on the whole people will feel that it is a more-than-fair trade. Almost everyone will happily accept the 'invasion of privacy' because it is not the State doing it to them; it is them doing it to themselves.

As the exploding supernet links-in increasingly sophisticated AI systems, the result is likely to feel so revolutionary, so liberating, so life-changing, that most of us will put up with its narrowcasting, the libelous nature of some areas, and the risk of major ID-theft caused by someone impersonating one of our multiple profiles. It is a price nearly every citizen of the international community will be willing to pay. Not quite the price

Side-effects

of Freedom, so much as the price of Free Entry. Of course we will expect the State to defend us when we are immersed within the virtual reality of the supernet. But the civil liberty we will mainly be demanding will *not* be privacy. It will be continued right of access.

A WORLD-ECONOMY DRIVEN BY AI AND THE SUPERNET

The net effect of Digitization augmented by Networking is a global economy driven by AI and the supernet – and inexplicable without them

THESE THEN ARE the combined thrusts of a couple of the dominant drivers of the world economy. Yet even only halfway through analyzing the power of the High-Tech launch engine it is nevertheless possible to make out some important aspects of its impact on our overall trajectory. There will be heavy use of virtual reality and augmented reality to supplement more traditional social interaction and to help compensate for the boredom felt by those trapped in more-disordered physical jobs where robots remain uneconomic, and to escape the stress felt by everyone from teachers and doctors to secretaries and call-center operatives who find that their roles are changing out of all recognition. Everywhere people will see varying degrees of AI-support in the form of intelligence-amplifiers and virtual assistants, right up to the superintelligences or very-fast intelligences used by the richest corporations and nations. And nearly all of the international community will have collective access to such an expanding archive of everything that is happening and has happened in the real world and virtual worlds that without AI support it will be impossible to make any sense of it.

Largely hidden, but intertwined throughout these images of the future, are the impacts of the third major exponential component of the High-Tech launch engine. Conceptually its operation is quite distinct from both Digitization and Networking, even though it plays a crucial role in amplifying the power of both. The focus of the next chapter, however, is not on the ways in which this third booster reinforces the thrusts that we have already discussed. Instead I will concentrate on how it substantially *alters* what otherwise would be the trajectory of the world economy because of the completely new opportunities that it opens up – which are largely unrelated to computing. In many ways, it is only because of

Digitization with Networking

Digitization and Networking that these breakthroughs will be possible. But the end-results will rival even AI and the supernet in terms of their impact on our lives. This third stage of our High-Tech propulsion is the apparently mundane trend of Miniaturization.

It is, in fact, a sleeping giant.

CHAPTER SUMMARY
NETWORKING

Networking will by 2040 lead to computers capable of human-like interaction and an internet a billion times more powerful than today's

Top-down Networking will by 2040 result in supercomputers 30,000 times more powerful than today's with human-level machine intelligence
- *Tightly-networked computer processors in the form of supercomputers permit the highest possible overall computing power to be gained from a given level of technology*
- *By 2040 supercomputers should be at least 30,000 times more powerful than the best of today and pass the so-called Turing Test for human-level machine intelligence*
- *Despite the likelihood of machine intelligence, the concept of a Singularity after which human progress accelerates beyond imagination is based on fundamental errors*
- *The strategic advantages of access to human-level AI will lead to a form of arms-race not only amongst Defense Departments but potentially also well-funded religions*
- *Corporations developing AI will focus on extremely-fast human-level intelligence that is easy to interact with rather than vastly-superior levels of machine intelligence*

Bottom-up Networking will by 2040 lead to 'ubiquitous computing' and a 'supernet' a billion times more powerful than today's internet
- *The concept of individual personal-computers will be replaced by so-called 'ubiquitous computing' in which almost every object contains an on-line processor*
- *Today's internet will continue to explode in terms of numbers of discrete devices and the increasing sophistication of those devices all linked in increasingly useful ways*

Chapter summary

Strong AI with the supernet will transform areas like education and health but also bring revolutions in virtual reality and social networking

- *Education goals will utterly change once most information is instantly available – and healthcare will likewise be transformed by on-line diagnosis and telemedicine*
- *Readily-affordable Virtual Reality systems will be addictive as computer-generated environments and even relationships become superior to those offered in the real-world*
- *Social networking systems will become immensely sophisticated as profile data is continuously mined and made available in real-time during real-world interactions*

Inevitable Networking side-effects will lead to polarized intolerance, loss of privacy and demands for legal Rights of Access to the supernet

- *The supernet will polarize intolerance as those holding unrepresentative views are nevertheless able to avoid much exposure to ideas other than those similar to their own*
- *Personal privacy will become far less about civil-liberties and much more about perceived fairness for supernet-users trading their privacy for free-access to providers*
- *As the supernet becomes increasingly crucial, the international community will demand that the rights of service-providers are curtailed to protect Rights of Access*

The net effect of Digitization augmented by Networking is a global economy driven by AI and the supernet – and inexplicable without them

MINIATURIZATION overview

Miniaturization offers nanotech breakthroughs ranging from cancer treatments to quantum computing – but not Replicators or 'grey goo'

- Despite counter-productive hype of the term 'nano', overall trends in Miniaturization are relatively-predictable and will be extraordinary

- Technology that is used to make computer-chips is leading to Top-Down manufacture of minute devices and eventually to Quantum Computers

- Technology previously associated with Biology and Chemistry is allowing Bottom-Up manufacture of smartparticles and exotic structures

- Most fears about nanotech are unfounded – nanobots will not turn the world to 'grey goo' and there will not be a 'post-scarcity economy'

- The net effect of Miniaturization reinforcing the otherwise-separate trends of Digitization and Networking will transform everyday-life

MINISCULE MACHINES...

...SMARTPARTICLES...

...EXOTIC STRUCTURES...

...QUANTUM COMPUTING...

THIRD-STAGE BOOSTER

MINIATURIZATION

WHY THE MINI PROVED SO GROOVY

The Miniaturization trend has become deeply embedded into modern society because manufacturers, distributors and consumers all benefit from the results

THE SLIGHT VIBRATION of a high-capacity iPod masks one of humanity's greatest mechanical achievements. Inside, a read-write head is flying over an undulating magnetic-disk so fast and so close that it is equivalent to a jumbo-jet skimming across rolling countryside at an altitude measured in centimeters. And that is just a consumer device. Today's most advanced hard-disk drives have a gap between the head and the disk-surface that is only twenty times the gap *between the atoms that make up the disk itself.* Each new generation of devices, that gap gets even smaller.

FLYING ACES

The read-write heads for the most advanced magnetic hard-disks now fly less than three billionths of a meter (3 nm) above the drive – that is about a thirty-thousandth of the thickness of a human hair.

It is all part of a Miniaturization trend that began accelerating in the 1950s at the start of the Space Race. By the 1960s the attractions of smallness were wowing the consumer market. It was not just the miniature Transistor Radio that caught the public imagination but also the iconic Mini – whether in the form of a car or a skirt. James Bond became synonymous with ultra-cool miniaturized gadgets. And everyday-people increasingly bought their music on small 45s instead of large LPs and played them on portable record players instead of large gramophones. It was all very alluring. It still is.

Developments despite hype

The point is that Miniaturization is not just attractive to those who want to launch something into outer-space. Achieving the same performance with less volume and weight is as convenient for average consumers as for rocket scientists. But there is more to it than that. In reality, as something gets smaller it is often possible to make it *better* as well. Quality and reliability may be higher. It may be possible to manufacture it more efficiently. Material-costs may be less. In addition, its smaller size usually makes it much easier and cheaper to ship and to use. It may operate faster or quieter. And, as with the mobile phone, after a device has been shrunk to an optimal size it may make sense to stop shrinking it and instead stuff it with increasingly complex features for the same price. Overall, the Miniaturization trend has become deeply embedded into modern society simply because manufacturers, distributors and consumers *all* benefit.

Yet even that is only part of the reason why this trend has taken hold so strongly within High-Tech. It is not just that Miniaturization can generate wins for everyone involved, but applied in the right way it creates a form of positive-reinforcement that is unique: Learn to make High-Tech smaller and you can use it to make measuring devices and manufacturing equipment that in turn let you make High-Tech even smaller – at the same time as it becomes better and generates ever-greater wins for everybody. As already covered on page 76, when applied to Digitization and Networking this approach is accelerating the global economy toward throwaway computers, sensors and displays that will routinely be embedded into everything from food-labels and pieces of clothing to envelopes and tickets. But where else is Miniaturization set to take the international community?

Many futurists have made alarming (and therefore very well publicized) claims about swarms of unbelievably small self-replicating devices eventually getting loose, resulting in human civilization being destroyed by 'grey goo'. I have worked with some of the experts researching in this area, and I have double-checked those claims. Others have prophesized that far-more-benign micromachines will soon lead to extraordinary medical advances. I have assessed those forecasts as well. But in order accurately to portray our most likely future, I have mainly had to focus on evaluating the large number of high-impact developments that – although in reality very likely – have often gained no widespread coverage whatsoever.

GETTING THE FUTURE YOU PAID FOR

Because of the high barriers against newcomers entering into Miniaturization developments, the direction of the trend is dictated by the major players that fund it

THE REASON WHY it is possible to be far more precise than many might think about where this particular trend is taking the world economy is that, below the surface, it is structurally very different to something like the growth of the internet. Back in the 1990s, almost anyone with a good idea for an on-line service, as well as many who did not even have that but did have loads of enthusiasm, could enter the market and see if anybody was interested in what they were offering. As a result, during those early stages, it was almost impossible to predict what internet entrepreneurs might come up with. After all, they were only really limited by their imaginations. Miniaturization is *not* like that. Even though, in theory, this trend could develop in utterly unpredictable ways – including the direction many sci-fi writers have predicted – the reality is that it is far more constrained than most forecasters have appreciated.

That is because the barriers to entering the Miniaturization market have become very high. Already, coming up with new designs demands an unusual blend of expensive, cross-disciplinary PhD-level expertise drawn from fields as wide-ranging as materials science, chemical synthesis and molecular biology, not to mention the more esoteric fields of quantum physics, photonics and nanofabrication. If entrepreneurs do not have access to such skills then they cannot even join this exclusive club. To have a hope of competing with other members, they need to spend a large fortune – with no guarantees that they will get a return on their investment. What is more, if some other company invents a really useful component or manufacturing technique, it will be patented. So a new entrant to the field will either be excluded from using that Intellectual Property, or they will have to pay to use it – which they will probably

Developments despite hype

choose to do because ultimately that will be cheaper than trying to develop an alternative that gets around the patent.

All this makes it far easier to predict where Miniaturization is headed: It is mainly going where it is being heavily funded to go. And long-term funding is dependent on the vested interests of a few large corporations (such as pharmaceutical multinationals and computer-chip manufacturers), start-ups funded by venture-capital corporations with very deep pockets, and government funding (especially relating to those departments interested in Defense, Intelligence, National Security, Energy and Healthcare).

The trend is also dependent on which of the richest nations have best anticipated how crucial the Miniaturization trend will be. For the last decade, the USA has been one of the heaviest investors, with a far more integrated research program than, for instance, the European Union. China is apparently spending less in absolute terms, but its top PhDs are on far lower salaries so the net effect is they are further ahead than it looks in terms of research power, and they have a stronger economy. As a result of all these factors, the default future from this trend is already far clearer than many people assume – and it is very different to what several forecasters have suggested.

Here is what is about to happen. Over the last few decades the general public has got used to the idea that clever chemistry has led to non-stick pans, gloss paints that can easily be washed off brushes, and matt varnish. Quite separately, everyone now takes for granted that miniscule inkjet printer-heads can fire droplets of ink so accurately and fast that they can print a whole page in only a few seconds. The Miniaturization trend over the next several decades is going to develop where these two fundamentally different approaches (chemistry and electromechanical engineering) meet in the middle. As a result, Miniaturization will open up radically new opportunities. Similarly to how Networking will simultaneously develop both Bottom-Up and Top-Down, so the prospects in Miniaturization occur where the two previously-very-different forms of bottom-up and top-down manufacturing (chemistry-based and engineering-based) increasingly overlap. In only a few years, the number of revolutionary breakthroughs generated from that intersection is set to explode.

THE HYPE OF NANOTECH

Political and commercial claims that nanotechnology will soon be a 'trillion dollar market' are
overstated and confusing – even though the field
will indeed prove crucial

FOR THE MOMENT at least, everyone is hyping 'nanotechnology'. In
essence this field is nothing more than building things at very small sizes –
measured in nanometers (billionths of a meter). The distance between
atoms in a solid is typically measured in tenths of a nanometer, so that
gives an idea of the scale on which the field is focused. And that is really all
that the term Nanotechnology means: Manufacturing and manipulating
materials and devices at the scale of atoms and molecules. The trouble is
that the word 'nanotech' is currently being grossly overused. It has become
an umbrella term that is often stuck over anything that is even loosely
connected to atomic effects in the hope of making it sound special.

THE DWARF KINGDOM

Nano- is simply the prefix in the metric system for 0.000000001 (in
other words, a billionth) derived from the Ancient Greek 'nanos'
meaning dwarf.

For example, medieval craftsmen made certain stained-glass windows by
coating the glass with incredibly fine particles of gold that were so small
they could not be seen but instead made the glass look red. These artisans
did not of course understand the physics of what they were doing, but
nevertheless, because the gold particles were in the nano range, this has
become a stock example of 'early nanotech'. And because there are now
computer microchips being manufactured in which some of the smallest
features are also in the nano range, many enthusiasts lump all this form of

top-down manufacturing into nanotech because it makes the field look much larger – though rather inconsistently they still call the products *micro*chips rather than *nano*chips.

Even more misleadingly, top government organizations (and journalists following their lead) routinely refer to nanotech as becoming a 'trillion dollar market' within a handful of years. But that estimate includes the full cost of every product that in any way *includes* any nanotech, however low the actual cost of that component. By the same logic, it should include the cost of medieval red glass. Such hype is a mistake that carries quite unnecessary risks of backfiring.

NANOTECH APPROACH TO MARKET EVALUATION

I once conducted a strategic analysis for a major corporation that made pigments that could be added to everything from paints to plastics. They wanted my team to tell them what the global market for the pigments was worth. If I had adopted the approach used by far-too-many government organizations to describe the supposed-size of the nanotech market, I would have given the CEO a figure equivalent to the cost of every pot of paint and colored plastic object sold in the world. But obviously that would have been absurdly misleading. His company's market was the pigment market. It did not sell paints or plastic. Likewise, if a 'nanotech' component is added to an expensive face cream to provide sun-protection, then it is the cost of the additive that should count toward the global market for nanotech, not the cost of the overall cosmetic.

Just as when some researchers back in the 1980s hyped that machine intelligence was 'just around the corner', there is a real risk that within a few years nanotech will be thought to have underperformed. Or, as happened with the term 'nuclear', nanotech will become overly associated with the negative connotations of some small part of it, and as a result the whole will be set back (just as fail-safe forms of nuclear power-generation have been). Either way, I suspect that the current fad for calling such a wide range of quite separate fields 'nanotech' will gradually lose its appeal. After all, it has become so very broad and confusing that most people –

MINIATURIZATION

including many of the journalists writing about it – do not really even understand the overall pattern of what is going on. Here, therefore, is a basic explanation.

WORLD-CLASS SCULPTURE IN SILICON

Conventional computer-chip manufacturing involves building 3-D sculptures of varying materials – but those techniques can equally well make other minute devices

THE FIRST SET of developments coincide with the direction that computer-chip manufacturing is progressing. This sort of 'top-down' technique involves diverse methods of depositing various kinds of material onto a base and then cutting away those parts that are not wanted – rather like a sculptor carving a statue from a block of stone. Repeat the process using different materials, and a chip-manufacturer can build up layer upon layer of a complex three-dimensional sculpture containing all sorts of different features. Up until now those 3-D sculptures have tended to be rather flat miniature-electronic components linked together in complex ways by pathways that conduct electricity. But there is no reason at all why this highly advanced form of manufacturing need be restricted to electronics alone.

It is relatively easy, for instance, to build a highly-reliable miniature accelerometer on a chip – that is how modern airbags are triggered in an automobile collision. It is also the way many computer games sense how a player is moving (although the more sophisticated way is to interpret a player's motions visually using a camera and pattern-recognition software). Over the next few decades, highly specific and sensitive sensors linked via the supernet will increasingly be attached to almost everything and test almost anything from automotive gas emissions to oxygen levels in a person's blood. But there is something far more sophisticated that is coming: a whole medical laboratory on a single chip.

HOW A LAB-ON-A-CHIP IMPROVES THE HEALTH OF SCIENCE

Potential developments such as a whole medical laboratory on a chip open the possibility of fundamental changes to both healthcare and how science itself advances

LAB-ON-A-CHIP DEVELOPMENTS BEGAN to take off as a result of the initial work on decoding the Human Genome, and now strong global interest stretches from the military to the health services. Technically it is actually quite complex because at the microscopic scale even very fluid liquids can move like thick treacle and not want to mix together. What is more, in the same way that the surface-tension of water allows an insect to skate over the surface of a pond without getting wet, it can also stop fluids going where the lab-on-a-chip designers want.

However, the whole discipline of 'microfluidics' is becoming very sophisticated with staggeringly small pumps and valves potentially able to channel very small samples to different parts of a chip. In parallel, microscopic biosensors are being developed that can be so specific that they can register only a few molecules of a particular substance. In due course, chips will be able to test for hundreds of things all at the same time, all from one sample. Within a couple of decades, expect doctors (and insurance companies) to be able cost-effectively to check most of your health-risk factors in one go – covering everything from predisposition to Alzheimer's to risks of various forms of heart disease. General healthcare will increasingly shift from cure to prevention, much as dentistry in advanced countries already has.

Around that same time, people living in developed countries can also expect to pop to the supermarket pharmacy to pick up one of a range of disposable Medical Test Kits, all of which work within seconds. The average person will be able to run their own Liver Function Test or check for HIV. Or they can opt for a broader-spectrum device that will test to see

Developments despite hype

if it can immediately tell them what is causing their raised temperature and headache, as well as whether they need to bother their doctor or whether they can more effectively (because it is faster and just as accurate) safely treat themselves with an automatically prescribed specific medication that has already been cross-checked against their medical records to maximize efficacy and minimize side-effects. Indeed, sometimes a test-kit may interface directly with a patient's previously implanted 'pharmacy on a chip' that, for instance, releases a varying cocktail of heart-related medication as body-conditions alter throughout the day.

As these last examples show, it will be very helpful for most of these lab-on-a-chip (and pharmacy-on-a-chip) systems to be linked to the supernet, just as already suggested on page 78. That way they can tie into the wealth of relevant information relating to the tests and become far more valuable than just sophisticated sensors alone. But that raises an amazing possibility. If there are hundreds of millions (and later billions) of different test results on-line, that is a vital data-source for medical research. If each specific test can be cross-correlated with the anonymous results of every associated medical treatment everywhere   that will fundamentally change researchers' understanding of healthcare. Major medical breakthroughs will be made. And if the same philosophy is adopted with all the other sensors connected to the supernet, then every field of science, technology and medicine will be revolutionized. That really will open the doors to a Global Renaissance.

THE WEIRD AND WONDERFUL WORLD OF QUANTUM COMPUTING

Miniaturization so small it can take advantage of counterintuitive Quantum Effects is funded to solve problems in cryptography but will also transform search algorithms

THERE IS A difficulty with synthesizing from countless sensors in the way that I just suggested. The challenge of searching through all the data sources on the supernet to discover previously unrecognized correlations is astronomical. With conventional approaches to supercomputing, even once those systems have passed the Turing Test, running such a search would take vastly too long to execute. It is a type of problem that although it is theoretically possible to solve, it is just not practical even if you use hugely more powerful versions of today's computers. Fortunately, a radical alternative is on its way, even though it is currently being funded for a *very* different purpose.

When bank customers send payment instructions over the internet their message is encrypted using a cyber-security system that would take even the fastest supercomputers so long to break that in practice it is completely impossible. Security Services are not that bothered about hacking into bank accounts – after all, if they ever need to know what suspects have been doing, they just have to ask the bank. But it is a valid concern that even though major governments own the most powerful computers that have ever existed, they can still never crack that type of encryption, even if it is being used by terrorists about to set off a bomb in a crowded city-centre. No conventional computer design can help them. That is why some governments are heavily funding research into a profoundly different approach: Quantum Computing.

If it were not for the Defense implications, this would probably remain one of those abstruse areas of theoretical physics that fascinates a handful of genius-level academics but is heavily underfunded, not least because no one offering grants can quite believe that the research proposal is for real. The reason why it could so easily have been passed over is that if you follow the top-down Miniaturization trend far enough, you find that it leads not just to computer chips made of very small components, but to computer chips in which special types of components can be made *so* small that they can take advantage of the so-called 'quantum effects' that occur when you approach the scale of atoms. And some of these phenomena are frankly bizarre.

A single very-small object that, as in the 'big' world, can either be in one state or the opposite state (say, On or Off), can in the quantum world also be in *both* states simultaneously. That is like being On *and* Off at exactly the same time. Even more confusingly, two objects that are physically separate can act as if they are connected (what Einstein called 'spooky action at a distance').

ENTANGLED GENIUS

Brilliant as Einstein was, he really did not like many of the implications of the new quantum theory proposed by his fellow-physicists. He assumed that eventually their probabilistic model of the universe would be found to be flawed. The concepts used in today's Quantum Computer designs were amongst Einstein's least favorites. 'Superimposition' (an object simultaneously possessing two or more values of something) was bad enough. But 'entanglement' (one object that although physically separated from another object cannot accurately be described without a full description of its partner – in other words, the two distinct objects acting as if they are invisibly linked) incurred his greatest wrath. He thought the idea was absurd and was caused by a yet-undiscovered mistake in his colleagues' mathematics. In reality, it appears that it was Einstein that in this case got his thinking completely entangled.

Extremely weird though all this is, the implications are that it is realistic to build a Quantum Computer that effectively explores lots of possible combinations of something all at the same time, and after a while can zero-in on the answer that is most likely to be correct. It sounds absurd, but in research labs the basic principles have already been proved. Now it is 'only' a problem of building complex systems based on those techniques. Despite what a few optimists suggest, from everything I know I expect it will take a few decades. There are severe challenges in stopping the quantum data getting corrupted by the environment. And completely new ways of programming will be involved. And developers will need far more effective ways of influencing and measuring the very quantum phenomena on which the computer depends. The field is in its infancy. But too much rides on it eventually maturing for any of the major nations to let their rivals get there first. Just as the Space Race effectively kicked off the Miniaturization trend, so the deeply-vested interests funding Quantum Computing are set pretty well to ensure that it arrives by 2040. This trend is parallel to, but largely separate from, research into human-level AI. Both may eventually arrive within the same decade but Quantum Computers will do very different things.

They will certainly break conventionally impenetrable codes – though, as might be expected, thanks to Defense funding, so-called 'quantum cryptography' has already been demonstrated as a truly-uncrackable alternative, so *that* cipher-war may never really be won. However, for the wider population, Quantum Computing will change their lives because of its ability to conduct otherwise-impossible searches on the supernet and discover relationships and correlations that could never otherwise be revealed. And, as will be disclosed in the subchapter about *The High-Tech route to Global Renaissance* (page 172), they will also be able to run such exceptionally sophisticated simulations of the real world that they will forever change how Humans interact with Nature.

BUILDING MOLECULES FROM THE BOTTOM-UP

Chemists have long known how to build simple molecules bottom-up using basic ingredients, and Biologists increasingly do the same for complex molecules like DNA

OVER THE NEXT few decades the 'top-down' approach to manufacturing will stretch closer and closer toward the realm of individual atoms and the quantum-effects they exhibit. But that is not the only way the Miniaturization trend is being realized. For billions of years biology has successfully been using a 'bottom-up' approach to manufacturing in which collections of atoms in the form of (sometimes very complex) molecules are combined together to form cells, and organs, and animals. Potentially critical errors in the manufacturing process sometimes occur – cancers are an example – but it is an impressive alternative to the approach used by microchip manufacturers.

What is more, the idea of using molecular building-blocks to create something that is not just huge in comparison with its components but is also immensely complex in structure and operation has a great advantage over the idea of somehow achieving the same top-down. The advantage is that science *knows* that it is possible to do because that is the process by which all human brains (the most complex objects in the known universe) have already successfully been constructed. It is only relatively recently that biologists have been able to manipulate complex molecules such as DNA, though chemists have been doing the same with far simpler molecules for hundreds of years. However, now that the Miniaturization trend has led to inspection devices that can for the first time reveal images of individual atoms, it has become far easier to understand what is actually going on.

NANOSCOPES

Because atoms are much smaller than the wavelength of visible light it is theoretically impossible to view them through an optical microscope, however powerful the lenses are made. Even the much higher frequencies used in electron-microscopes can only reveal very large molecules. But research in the 1980s led to the Scanning Tunneling Microscope that routinely takes advantage of quantum effects to reveal (and even manipulate) individual atoms. Today's research for alternative imaging approaches includes techniques such as Magnetic Resonance Force Microscopy, which conceptually is like the MRI in a hospital – just ten billion times more sensitive.

From transparent sun-block to effective cancer treatments

Miniscule particles and ultrathin coatings have special properties for sunblock-creams, self-cleaning windows, coatings for medical implants and cancer treatments

AT THE NANO scale, biology and chemistry as well as physics all tend to look different. For a start, very small objects have a huge surface area compared with their volume. So if a lump of material is broken down into very small particles, vastly more of the material's surface will be in contact with its surroundings – whether that is air or something else. Wheat grains are pretty stable, but fine flour wafting around in a warehouse can explode. And nanoparticles are very much smaller than that. As a result, even if materials-scientists do not really do any bottom-up manufacturing to speak of, but instead just play around with basic very-small building blocks, they already get new characteristics just because of the changed geometry. That on its own is very useful for things like catalysts (substances that change the speed of chemical reactions) because they become more effective the more of their surface that is exposed. That is why automobile catalytic-converters are full of a honeycomb of material.

But it gets far more intriguing than that. At the nano scale the laws of quantum physics (how the universe operates across very small distances) start to dominate. I have already touched on some of the weirder effects in reference to Quantum Computers, but those were phenomena that humans can never experience directly. There are others. Materials can lose all electrical resistance. Opaque materials can become invisible. Remember how strong sunblock-cream used to be a pasty white colour? The reason why the latest creams are transparent is that the same sunblock material is now in particles that are so small they have effectively disappeared, even though they still have the same effect as before.

MINIATURIZATION

Naturally, nano-scale building blocks do not only have to be particles. They can be filaments, with one dimension vastly longer than the other two. Or they can be sheets, maybe only a molecule thick. If that one-molecule-thick sheet is attached to the surface of something else then it becomes a coating on that other material – the first step to a process of bottom-up manufacturing. In fact, that is how the latest generation of self-cleaning windows, scratch-resistant sunglasses, pearlescent paints and non-reflective surfaces all work. According to the hype-definition they are all examples of nanotechnology. More helpfully, they are early examples of the increasingly sophisticated coatings that will eventually be applied to an incredibly wide range of objects affecting every aspect of people's lives.

Medical implants, for instance, will be coated to be more hardwearing and corrosion resistant (inside the human body is a surprisingly hostile environment). Implants will also be coated to hide them from the body's defenses so as to avoid being attacked as foreign invaders. Bones and artificial joints will be coated to help them knit together in a way that never happens with conventional implants. However, one of the most exciting of the coating applications is, of all things, in drug delivery. The classic problem of treating things like tumors is to kill only the cancerous cells and no others. To do that, oncologists need to concentrate some pretty dangerous medication at the site of the tumor and nowhere else. To avoid what can be horrible side-effects they then ideally keep administering low doses of the drug over a long period. And they try to achieve all that without triggering the patient's immune system.

But bottom-up manufacturing addresses the problem in a very different way. The technique involves building lots of sophisticated nanoparticles all about a thousandth the diameter of a human hair – that is small enough that once injected into a patient's blood stream they can be carried throughout the whole body. The first stage of the manufacturing process is to make the core of the nanoparticle out of chemotherapy-drug molecules trapped in what effectively is a biodegradable sponge that once inside the body will gradually break down over several days and slowly release the drug. The next manufacturing stage is to coat each spherical core with a special substance that will stop the patient's immune system from recognizing the particle as a foreign object and destroying it as it otherwise would. The last stage is to add a final coat of special molecules that will *only* attach to the particular type of tumor cells that the treatment is designed to destroy.

Bottom-up

Treatment simply involves injecting the complex nanoparticles near the tumor. They float around, unattacked by antibodies, until they come across any of the specified type of cancer cells, and then they latch on. Slowly the nanoparticles break down, releasing medication in the optimal way. Already there are human clinical trials underway applying this technique to treat prostate cancer. But there seems no reason to suppose that similar kinds of approach will not potentially work for nearly all solid tumors.

Unless something really unanticipated blocks progress, expect an increasing number of cancers to become fully treatable over the next decades. There is unlikely ever to be a single cure for cancer because 'cancer' is an umbrella term that covers innumerable types of uncontrolled division of cells, and there are very many different causes – not least old age. However, many of us will gradually lose our collective fear of cancers as, one by one, different examples of the disease become completely manageable and even curable. Ironically, these final battles in the war on cancer may be decided less by a last-minute rush of biological advances and more by the steady progress of Miniaturization.

SUPERHARD, SUPERSTRONG, SUPERMAGNETIC

Exotic superhard, superstrong or supermagnetic materials will lead to incredible consumer innovations and major breakthroughs in solar-energy and electricity storage

THE CONCEPT OF bottom-up manufacturing also offers the promise of creating new substances that are rare or simply do not occur naturally at all. Materials that are superhard, superstrong, supermagnetic, and so on. It all started with carbon atoms. Until a few decades ago it was thought that pure carbon came in only two forms: graphite and diamond. Their properties are so different because of the way the atoms are organized – with graphite they are layered in geometrically regular one-atom-thick sheets of 'graphene' that can slide over each other, but in diamond the atoms are locked rigidly together in a 3-D crystal structure.

SHEETS OF PENCIL

Graphene is an amazing substance, although it is actually the material in a pencil lead. A single-atom thick, at the atomic level it is structured like the hexagons in chicken netting. It is incredibly strong, is a good thermal and electrical conductor, and has potential to be used for a wide variety of electronic components far faster than those of today. It also has some rather unusual properties. For example, even though a graphene membrane blocks all gases (including helium, which is normally very hard to stop leaking), water-vapor passes through it as if nothing were there. That makes room-temperature distillation possible. Already, vodka has been made higher proof. In the future, drinking water could be extracted from the sea or from polluted wells.

Then, twenty-five years ago, a laboratory made the first 'buckyball'. It was like a hollow sphere made of exactly sixty carbon atoms. And its properties were nothing like graphite *or* diamond. Then someone managed to make what became known as 'carbon nanotubes' – which were basically like buckyballs that had not closed up at the top and bottom so instead had formed minute cylinders of graphene (in other words, carbon atoms in an arrangement that makes them look like a thin tube of chicken netting).

BUCKYBALLS

Correctly termed 'buckminsterfullerene C_{60}' a buckyball is shaped like a soccer ball made up of twenty hexagons and twelve pentagons, with a carbon atom at each point – sixty in total. It was named after the architect Richard Buckminster Fuller, because its structure was so similar to the geodesic domes he devised. The term 'fullerene' is now used to describe the whole family of similarly structured forms that were later discovered – such as C_{70} and C_{80}.

These nanotubes were much stronger and stiffer than any other substance ever discovered, about a hundred times stronger by weight than steel. And they could conduct heat and electricity vastly better than materials such as copper. Then someone managed to make carbon nanotubes that were like one tube inside the other. These had even more intriguing properties. And so developments continue.

ABBREVIATED NANOTUBES

The term 'Carbon Nanotube' is sometimes abbreviated to CNT – although the scientific press these days commonly just uses NT (primarily because researchers are distinguishing between 'single-walled' and 'multi-walled' carbon nanotubes by using the nomenclature SWNT and MWNT).

MINIATURIZATION

Around the world, huge sums are now being invested into working out how to make enough of these sorts of new materials and then turn them into products that the global economy will want to pay for. Initially, throughout this current decade, the general public is likely to see more on the new-materials side of things than fundamentally new products. The military already have high hopes for nanotubes woven into clothing that offer superior protection against gunfire. And equivalent composite materials on armored vehicles would be incredibly strong and light. Those are two of many reasons why funding of these kinds of development is relatively immune to economic downturns.

By 2020, such composite materials will be moving into commercial aircraft construction with great benefits for fuel efficiency. Then they will be found appearing in automotive designs, offering higher safety with greater fuel-saving. Out of sight, at about the same time, far stronger magnets than ever existed before are likely to find their way into electric motors and power generators, making them much more efficient. And specialized analytical equipment such as hospital MRI scanners will move into a new league. Flat artificial 'metamaterials' will act as optically perfect lenses. Special filters will become available – for instance to purify contaminated water and make it safe to drink, or to scrub air free of pollutants.

Gradually the public will see radically new consumer products coming available. Amazingly clear and large displays the size of walls that can still be viewed in direct sunlight. Windows that can be switched to whatever level of brightness you want. Wall coverings that act as loud speakers. Wallpaper that can be changed to whatever colour and pattern you choose. Almost any surface being capable of being turned into a light-source. They have all been seriously considered already. Then there is Energy. There are strong hopes in some industries (leading to major concerns in others) that radically new types of materials will lead to very efficient and relatively inexpensive photocells that can convert unprecedented amounts of sunshine into commercial amounts of electric power. There are also largely separate activities aimed at using other types of radically new materials to *store* electricity far more efficiently than is currently possible with existing battery or fuel-cell technology.

These are not the new-generation lightweight batteries for things like electric cars, which will increasingly become available this decade. Instead, these are industrial-scale electrical storage devices for commercial solar-power stations – as well as other forms of renewable-power generation such as wind and tidal – that can store huge amounts of electricity for use overnight, or when the wind drops, or during the turn of the tide. I have had long discussions about all this with many of the corporations involved. My conclusion is that, despite a lot of enthusiasm in some quarters, we should not expect these developments for another couple of decades. At the earliest. The technical breakthroughs required are themselves daunting, though very likely in due course. However, what will delay everything is that for the technology to have a major impact requires massive infrastructural change. And, for primarily commercial reasons, there will be very strong forces amongst certain oil and energy producers that will potentially resist every one of those changes each step of the way.

WHAT YOU HAVE AUTHORITATIVELY BEEN TOLD — WRONGLY

Well-respected scientists, best-selling authors and influential futurists have made claims about nanotech-devices building everyday objects and the dangers of nanobots

THE FOLLOWING IS what the public has been told by various scientists, authors, and futurists: *'In the same way that top-down manufacturing techniques like those used by computer-chip manufacturers are already sculpting features so small that they are well within the nano range, the same devices could be manufactured bottom-up, molecule by molecule. But that is just the start. It automatically follows that only a few decades later members of the public will be able just to dial-up any object they want – such as food or clothes – and it will be fabricated for them. Just like the Replicator in the later versions of Star Trek. Nothing will be scarce anymore. In fact, because of their simple and regular structure, it will be far easier to fabricate diamonds than hamburgers. By around 2040, the fundamentals of the global economy will have been obliterated.'* At least, that is what the public has authoritatively been told.

It has also been told that: *'If top-down manufacturing can build miniaturized lab-on-a-chip devices, then bottom-up manufacturing can likewise create unbelievably small machines. After all, the cells in muscle-fiber are microscopic machines that contract when stimulated in the right way. Spermatozoa can swim in a chemically determined direction and then burrow into an egg cell. Human beings are already full of microscopic machines. In the future, medical-technologists will be able to build nano-scale robots – 'nanobots' – each designed to build many more nanobots, molecule by molecule, using the raw materials of their surroundings. Large numbers of these self-replicating nanobots can then be injected into the bloodstream to seek out damaged cells and repair them. Each device can easily have computing capability on board, as well as a way of communicating with fellow devices and impacting its environment. And each can draw its power from its surroundings. Just as with armies of ants, the coordinated behavior of a very large number of these nanobots together will be vastly more impressive than any one alone. Within only a few decades, nanobots will effectively make the human-race immortal. But there is a risk. If swarms of these self-replicating, self-powering nanobots get loose, they could attack the human race and eventually turn the whole world into a Grey Goo.'* At least, that is what the public has authoritatively been told. But *none* of the developments are going to turn out that way.

How 'Grey Goo' Got Lost in a Filing Cabinet

The concept of the threat of 'grey goo' is a leftover from research ideas of the 1980s that have long been superseded and the risks anyway were never well-founded

FOR A START, the idea of grey goo came from some research ideas in the 1980s about how bottom-up manufacturing might work. But by the 1990s that whole avenue of research had been pretty well abandoned. It became clear that rather than somehow designing self-replicating nanobots that could spawn a clone army, it would actually be a lot easier to build them using the nanotechnology equivalent of an automotive assembly-line. In terms of efficiency, Henry Ford basically got it right with his manufacturing approach for the Model T. Once a given approach gets established (whether it is automobile production techniques or the QWERTY keyboard-layout or the reciprocating internal-combustion engine) after a while it becomes very difficult for another approach to muscle in. For the last ten years, all the big funding for nanotech has ignored the self-replicating route. By now it would cost an unaffordable investment to try to make up for the lost time. And anyway, such an attempt would be very unlikely ever to catch up with the continuing advances being made using other techniques.

Even if they did, at that size the nanobots would not have the power to go far or fast (any more than sperm can), and every moment in the outside world they would risk being eaten and dissolved by everyday bacteria and fungi. Anyway, as an obvious precaution, their limited computer programming would as standard contain safeguards against unanticipated behavior, such as an automatic time-out if they did not receive a regular instruction-update or perhaps access to a rare molecule introduced into their immediate surroundings.

GENESIS OF THE NANOBOTS

The infamous term 'Grey Goo' was coined in the mid-1980s by Dr. Eric Drexler, one of the influential pioneers of nanotechnology. At the time it seemed a very reasonable concern to raise about nanobots, although its underlying assumptions subsequently caused great controversy. In a set of published articles and open letters starting in 2001, Nobel prize-winning chemist Dr. Richard Smalley took fundamental issue with Drexler over the practicality of ever building self-replicating nanobots at all.

If a malicious group managed to override these protections, any nanobot could in reality be instantaneously disabled by a mere spark, just as the static electricity someone can pick up from simply walking across a carpet is sufficient to fuse the circuitry of a modern computer chip if they touch it without being grounded to earth. A strong electromagnetic pulse would knock-out a whole swarm, however large. Basically, at whichever level the scare-story is viewed, uncontrollable nanobots may be good science-fiction, but they are bad science. The idea that originally spawned grey goo is currently locked away in some old slightly dusty research-archive filing cabinets. And the world has moved on.

3-D PRINTING – BUT NOT MOLECULAR-LEVEL REPLICATORS

The idea of a molecular-level Replicator that can manufacture everyday-objects may forever remain impractical for most applications – however 3-D printing will have a huge impact

WHAT ABOUT THE idea of the universal Replicator and civilization being forced into a 'post-scarcity' economy? For a start, it is not at all clear that it will *ever* be practical. The energy-levels needed to make a reasonably-sized object, for instance, might be prohibitive. On top of that, no one really has the slightest idea how even to approach the design challenge. But leaving concerns about mere things like the laws of physics to one side for the moment, there is still no way that any of this will happen by 2040. Or 2050. It is the 'robots doing the cleaning' fallacy again. Even if a Replicator was theoretically achievable within thirty years, that does not mean it has the slightest chance of being economically justifiable. The huge research costs would need to be clawed back, so each patented Replicator would be very expensive, and the early ones would be charged out at a premium. The royalties for the complex copyrighted software needed for replicating a given object would have to be paid each time. And there would also be no escaping a very high electricity bill.

If people want food and clothes in 2040, it will be a lot easier simply to order conventional versions on the supernet. Potential investors into Replicator research know perfectly well that even in thirty years, and even despite drought and land depletion, it will still be cheaper – *very, very much cheaper* – to grow food and weave clothes than to build them atom by atom. That is not a good sales pitch. They will pass on the funding opportunity. And thank goodness a Replicator is not realistic, because otherwise the disruption caused by suddenly breaking those massively entrenched aspects of the global economy that relate to conventional agriculture and manufacture would be utterly devastating. Indeed, if there ever was a risk of that, politicians at a global level would almost certainly legislate to control the Replicator's introduction. Their prime responsibility is, after all, to protect their respective economies. And it no longer suits anyone to devastate the global economy. The long and short of it is that if some type of extremely-specialized molecular-level Replicator ever does get built, it will be designed to fabricate ever-more-outlandish nanotechnology materials and devices that otherwise would be impossible – things like the next generation of ultra-sophisticated computer chips for super-intelligent computing. Objects for which customers will be willing to pay a *very* hefty premium.

In contrast, various techniques of '3-D printing' are showing great promise and are already widely used in industry for rapid-prototyping. These computer-based techniques create layer upon layer of material to build a potentially-highly-complex object. There are many approaches being tried, but they all tend to build up one thin slice of the cross-section of an object after another – either by solidifying bits of a special polymer or else by depositing a thin layer of material in similar ways to how the various types of electronic printer deposit ink. Already, 3 D printing has been used to construct complicated inert implants to replace lost bone in human patients; in due course it may even prove practical to 'print' biological organs using living cells.

Despite the hype, however, many everyday objects will still be far cheaper to produce using advanced high-volume production techniques – just as it is cheaper for a newspaper publisher to print your copy of a high-circulation color-supplement than it would be for you (once you included the cost of expensive home-printer inks and consumables as well as a royalty fee for the magazine content) to print a copy yourself. Whatever overexcited futurologists claim, the concept of 'economies of scale' does not disappear just because a new form of one-off manufacturing appears – the trade-offs merely realign. Only if the full cost of a 3-D-print is the *same as or lower than* an equivalent quality (and maybe also cachet) of conventionally-manufactured object do the rules radically change. And that is very unlikely to occur by 2040. Instead, we may 'print' some objects at home. But we will continue to order most online.

LEGITIMATE CONCERNS OVER NANOPARTICLES

Although all the well-publicized scare stories about nanotech are false, there are valid concerns over possible health-risks from nanoparticles and other exotic materials

FOR THE RECORD, I do consider there are some valid concerns about nanotechnology, but they certainly have nothing to do with Nanobots or Replicators. Instead they are to do with size. Science simply does not have enough experience of the impact on humans or animals of large numbers of incredibly small particles if accidently breathed in or left on skin too long – let alone if injected into the bloodstream and so introduced into the brain. There may be nothing to worry about. But that is what was originally thought about asbestos as a building material and thalidomide as a treatment for morning-sickness. Well-funded research around the globe is already checking out these sorts of concerns. However, as already mentioned, the behavior of even familiar materials can totally change when they are miniaturized to the nano scale. As a result, governments should not be lulled into a false sense of security. Any new objects of nano size should be treated with the same respect normally reserved for new chemicals and biological agents.

MINIATURIZATION REINFORCING DIGITIZATION AND NETWORKING

The net effect of Miniaturization reinforcing the otherwise-separate trends of Digitization and Networking will transform everyday-life

EVEN IF THERE are not yet any real signs of commercially-viable bottom-up molecular assemblers, the impact of the Miniaturization trend throughout the next thirty years will nevertheless be extraordinary. As already highlighted, Miniaturization is currently strongly reinforcing the Digitization and Networking trends and setting the global economy on a course toward ubiquitous computing embedded into everything that people own – all interlinked via the supernet – leading amongst many other things to early detection of disease and a shift in emphasis for healthcare from cure to prevention.

As we have also seen, Miniaturization is set to eradicate most cancers, provide safe and affordable drinking water, and introduce lighter and stronger materials everywhere. And the default future is that by 2040 the international community will have economic solar-power and (thanks to quantum computing) unimaginable search-capability on the supernet that, combined with human-level AI, will result in escalating scientific, technological, medical, sociological and artistic breakthroughs. Yet even the breathtaking trajectory achieved by these first three accelerating boosters of our future is itself being relentlessly steepened even further by the fourth stage of the High-Tech launch engine.

In many ways, this is the oldest and most mysterious trend of them all.

MINIATURIZATION

Miniaturization offers nanotech breakthroughs ranging from cancer treatments to quantum computing – but not Replicators or 'grey goo'

Despite counter-productive hype of the term 'nano', overall trends in Miniaturization are relatively-predictable and will be extraordinary

▪ *The Miniaturization trend has become deeply embedded into modern society because manufacturers, distributors and consumers all benefit from the results*

▪ *Because of the high barriers against newcomers entering into Miniaturization developments, the direction of the trend is dictated by the major players that fund it*

▪ *Political and commercial claims that nanotechnology will soon be a 'trillion dollar market' are overstated and confusing – even though the field will indeed prove crucial*

Technology that is used to make computer-chips is leading to Top-Down manufacture of minute devices and eventually to Quantum Computers

▪ *Conventional computer-chip manufacturing involves building 3-D sculptures of varying materials – but those techniques can equally well make other minute devices*

▪ *Potential developments such as a whole medical laboratory on a chip open the possibility of fundamental changes to both healthcare and how science itself advances*

▪ *Miniaturization so small it can take advantage of counterintuitive Quantum Effects is funded to solve problems in cryptography but will also transform search algorithms*

Chapter summary

Technology previously associated with Biology and Chemistry is allowing Bottom-Up manufacture of smartparticles and exotic structures

- *Chemists have long known how to build simple molecules bottom-up using basic ingredients, and Biologists increasingly do the same for complex molecules like DNA*
- *Miniscule particles and ultrathin coatings have special properties for sunblock-creams, self-cleaning windows, coatings for medical implants and cancer treatments*
- *Exotic superhard, superstrong or supermagnetic materials will lead to incredible consumer innovations and major breakthroughs in solar-energy and electricity storage*

Most fears about nanotech are unfounded – nanobots will not turn the world to 'grey goo' and there will not be a 'post-scarcity economy'

- *Well-respected scientists, best-selling authors and influential futurists have made claims about nanotech-devices building everyday objects and the dangers of nanobots*
- *The concept of the threat of 'grey goo' is a leftover from research ideas of the 1980s that have long been superseded and the risks anyway were never well-founded*
- *The idea of a molecular-level Replicator that can manufacture everyday-objects may forever remain impractical for most applications – however 3-D printing will have a huge impact*
- *Although all the well-publicized scare stories about nanotech are false, there are valid concerns over possible health-risks from nanoparticles and other exotic materials*

The net effect of Miniaturization reinforcing the otherwise-separate trends of Digitization and Networking will transform everyday-life

SIMULATION overview

Simulation will support fundamental and sweeping advances that lead to almost limitless electricity and maybe almost limitless life-extension

- Modeling the world with Simulation is the best way of transforming cutting-edge science into radical technology and life-changing medicine

- Fusion Power has an extraordinary potential to solve future energy demands but the chances of it being ready in time depend on Simulation

- Molecular Biology will totally change what it means to be alive – but although it can be immensely positive it will become an ethical minefield

- The net effect of Simulation with Miniaturization, Networking and Digitization will potentially lead to an unprecedented Global Renaissance

WORLD MODELING...

   ...FUSION POWER...

      ...MOLECULAR BIOLOGY...

         ...LIFE-CHANGING THERAPIES...

FOURTH-STAGE BOOSTER

SIMULATION

THE ANCIENT ART OF MODELING THE UNIVERSE

Although it is now underpinned by the other three High-Tech trends, Simulation is an ancient trend deeply embedded into the global economy and is largely unstoppable

THE SIMULATION BOOST is already deeply coordinated with the previous three thrusts of the High-Tech engine. Designing new integrated-circuits, for instance, has become so complicated and expensive that, long before a physical prototype can be built, every characteristic must first be planned, modeled, tested and refined by simulation on a computer. Today's sophisticated industrial robots simulate complex movements before executing them, and tomorrow's robot cars will depend on constantly updating a virtual model of the real-world within their on-board computers. The automobiles themselves during their design stages will have been repeatedly crash-tested in virtual reality, rather than in the physical world using expensive prototypes and inadequate crash-dummies.

Already, surgeons are able to simulate a patient's heart to decide where best to place a pacemaker before implanting it. And for several decades, some AI research has involved simulating the operation of individual neurons within biological brains; some current research is aimed at eventually simulating a whole human brain. Most advances in nanotechnology are now only possible because researchers can simulate the behavior of atoms and molecules on computer. And Quantum Computers are seen as worthy of major state-funding because, in addition to their lure of code-breaking and complex searching, they potentially offer advances in simulation (not least for war-gaming, defense-system design and military-personnel training) that are currently almost inconceivable.

The underlying explanation for this interdependence of Simulation with Digitization, Networking and Miniaturization, and the reason why it is realistic to forecast where the trend is headed, is that Simulation is very much more deeply embedded into modern society – and therefore its overall direction is far more predictable – that most people assume. Under different guises, the foundations of the Simulation trend have been around a very long time. A major stimulus for electrical computing was simulating artillery fire so gunners could be more accurate. Today everyone views analog clocks as devices to tell the time, but that is only because they accurately simulate the rotation of the earth. Many old grandfather clocks also simulated the phases of the moon. Scientific instruments thousands of years ago simulated the movements of the sun, moon, planets and stars.

GREEK LOVE OF WISDOM

One of the earliest genius thinkers is today known by the name of Thales from the city of Miletus (in modern-day Turkey). He refused to accept mystical explanations for natural phenomena. Out of this concept grew what the Ancient Greeks called 'love of wisdom' – that is the English translation but in Greek it sounded like *philo-sophia*. This early modeling of reality was tremendously enhanced by the invention a few hundred years earlier of the very first complete alphabet, which allowed any language to be written down, even if it was not Greek, using a combination of only twenty-four squiggles. It did not require years of training as a scribe to learn the alphabet, opening up the possibility of almost anyone writing their ideas down and making them public so that they could be debated, understood, added to *and corrected*. It was the beginning of the Scientific Method that eventually created our modern world.

Yet the foundations of the Simulation trend are even older and deeper than those early mechanical devices. The beginnings stretch back at least 2,600 years to when the earliest Greek philosophers asked, possibly for the first time in human history, if it was possible to create models of the universe that explained natural phenomena in terms of matter and physical forces rather than the action of the gods. That idea of modeling reality was a staggering leap of intellect that elsewhere at the time simply did not make sense to people. To the rest of the world it was a meaningless quest because a rich cocktail of Magic and Religion explained everything – and therefore why *should* there even be any models to discover?

In many ways, today's Simulation trend is a direct legacy from the ancient modeling of those Greek intellectual rebels. And its impact is set to be just as revolutionary because it allows scientists, engineers and doctors to model existence – indeed the whole universe – as never before. They can create inner worlds that mirror our world outside. But they can also do far more. As Masters of their Universes they can explore exactly how their doppelganger creations work, how things would alter if aspects were changed, *and* how best to reproduce those discoveries in the outer world. Simulation is already very much more than just a computer-based form of modeling; it has become by far the most effective means available of transforming cutting-edge Science into radical Technology and life-changing Medicine. And that makes it almost unthinkably powerful.

COSMETIC-SOFTWARE AND OTHER FALSE SENSES OF SECURITY

Advances driven by Simulation will revolutionize almost every aspect of society – although the most far-reaching impacts will be to Fusion Power and Molecular Biology

AS ALREADY DETAILED in the subchapter about *Why Artificial Reality will become so addictive* (page 83), thanks to Simulation virtual-reality on the supernet will become extremely sophisticated and will in effect offer the opportunity to improve upon reality. Computer games will soon be extraordinary. Hollywood special-effects, even of 'humans', will become indistinguishable from the real thing and will totally change the economics of A-list movie stars and the film industry generally. The same will happen to the stars of the pop-music industry, especially those leveraging the music-video market. Apart from anything, it will allow performers to adopt whatever image their producers believe will sell best. Indeed, it will allow the *same* performer to adopt as many persona (aimed at as many narrow niches) as the market can handle.

Television budgets will allow production values that previously were only possible with cinema-release projects. And those categories of human performers that are not gradually replaced by simulated alternatives – all politicians and most real-time presenters are safe – will increasingly be able to request that television production crews apply carefully-personalized 'cosmetic software' to the broadcast to remove wrinkles and thicken hair during live interviews, just as Hollywood can already do for movies. Commercial training systems such as flight-simulators, virtual military-exercises, teaching for hospital A&E and surgery will all become highly advanced. The raw data from hospital CT and MRI scans will be transformed into immensely sophisticated and detailed 3-D representations that reveal far more than would possibly be visible in the real world. Meanwhile, computer-based modeling will lead to everything from less-congested roads (or at least less congested than they otherwise would be) to far more effective political spin and economic interventions, national security-profiling and war strategy, climate policy and commodity prices.

Despite an inevitably slow transformation of the formal education process, unauthorized but highly-effective educational-simulation packages – often written by students themselves – will become so commonly shared over the supernet that many children and students will simply use them unofficially, because they find them far more useful (or at least interesting) than the 'old-fashioned' syllabus being taught by 'out-of-date' teachers in the classroom. By around 2030, much of the education system will find itself always lagging behind, trying to control a process that is no longer under its direct influence, increasingly dragged along by its students,

Meteorology has already made major strides in weather-forecasting, and local forecasts will further improve in accuracy even though there are theoretical limits to any weather forecast of more than a few days, especially in regions of unsettled weather. Bankers, financiers and economists will continue to develop ever-more-sophisticated simulations of the global economy. But just as with attempts to model climate change, such simulations are only as good as the equations on which they are based. That is because, unlike simulating the physics of solid objects (for instance for automotive design or civil-engineering projects), or even of nuclear particles (for designing Quantum Computers or exotic nanomaterials), no one knows all the correct ways to approximate the intricacies of hugely-complex systems like economies, or social structures, or earthquake zones, or worldwide atmospheres.

As a result, although there will be dramatic improvements in the speed with which all these sorts of simulations can be run – eventually they will be able to operate continuously in real-time – even by 2040 they will still be open to major errors. In essence, the more that they simulate 'business as usual' the better it will be possible to fine-tune them so that most of the time they correspond with reality. But even if the simulations eventually become self-correcting (refining their own models to match better what actually occurs) there will still be no reason to believe that those models are the *same* as the real-world. All simulations, however well accepted they become, nevertheless offer a potentially false sense of security when used to model events outside the norm.

Transforming science

As an example, scientists have spent more than two millennia creating models that are good approximations to what actually happens – we call them Hypotheses, Theories and Laws. But science has also spent those same two millennia correcting and fine-tuning the models and sometimes completely throwing them out and starting again, which is what happened to Newtonian physics around a century ago when it began to be replaced by Quantum physics as the way to model extremely small phenomena. Simulations of very complex systems are *always* approximations. That means they can give incorrect answers that even experts may not realize are wrong. In 2040 and beyond, that risk will necessarily remain.

However, despite such inherent problems, there are two fields in which Simulation is set to revolutionize the world economy utterly. Those two sets of innovations will rock our world. And to reflect that, I have focused most of the remainder of this chapter exclusively on them: Fusion Power and Molecular Biology.

WHEN THERE ARE NOT ENOUGH ALTERNATIVE ENERGIES

Despite strong pressures for economies to move away from oil-dependency, even a balance of alternatives is unlikely to satisfy the world's energy requirements by 2040

IT IS IN nuclear physics that the Simulation trend is set to make one of its biggest impacts on this century. Few people realize that the earliest computer simulations were in fact used to model the detonation of nuclear explosions, initially as part of the top-secret World War II Manhattan Project in the USA that led to the Atomic Bomb (as dropped on Japan) and later to the far more powerful Hydrogen Bomb. Before 2040, Simulation will again help unleash the formidable power of the H-bomb. But this time, Simulation's contribution will be completely benign. It will be all about *containing* the explosion.

With public concerns over global warming combining with fuel-price hikes and worries about long-term availability of oil, most governments around the world currently feel it is very important to make sure they are seen to encourage technology that exploits renewable energy sources such as solar and wind. What all the governments know, however, is that the classic examples of renewable energy are not guaranteed to be sufficient long-term solutions. As I will cover on page 188, although few politicians publicize the fact, it is far from clear whether future-generation nanotech solar cells and power storage, for instance, will in fact become viable options in time, before rising costs of oil extraction from less-economic sources – or, possibly far earlier, political problems – force a major shift away from oil-dependency.

What is more, many major economies have neither the climate nor, in many cases, enough unpopulated and uncultivated land for a sufficient number of solar farms, even if nanotech in due course makes them more efficient and more economically attractive. After all, however efficient the collection technology, the minimum area needed is ultimately dictated by the physics of sunshine. And distributing electricity over long distances from solar farms in other countries results in major losses. Wind farms can carry a high social cost. Tidal energy is of little use to countries with limited coastline. And all these forms of power-generation can (despite economies of scale) cost *more and more* as the number of generators is increased, because the best or cheapest sites tend to have already been used up with the first set of generators. As a result of all these factors, most governments are spreading their bets.

In addition to encouraging energy-efficiency measures, politicians make a big deal out of Green Technologies such as techniques for cutting CO_2 emissions. Using the argument that 'It's better in the long run than oil or coal,' many governments that previously cut back their nuclear-power station programs are beginning to reinstate them – albeit with extra scrutiny as a result of the tsunami at Fukushima power-plant. Yet, even assuming that all these plans are realized on schedule (which from past experience of major civil-engineering projects seems over-optimistic), those politicians looking ahead past their current retirement dates see that there may still be a major problem. The sums may still not add up.

As detailed on page 189, by 2040 there will be a far larger world population with, on average, much higher expectations. And it is not at all clear that projected energy demands can be satisfied using only the renewable and conventional power-generation facilities being planned. Even if high-efficiency solar cells get developed in time and all the proposed new nuclear power-plants (and oil- and coal-fired generators) get built, the general population may well want much more. As a result, many of the richest governments have clubbed together to back a very-long-term answer. They are allocating more research funds into it than any other rival approach. In fact, they have been quietly channeling major funding to it for fifty years.

THE SECRET HOPE OF FUSION POWER

Research into Fusion Power – which is hoped to be commercialized around 2040 – is quietly but heavily being funded by international consortia and is totally dependent on Simulation

MOST OF THE general public, and certainly the average politician, has not the slightest idea what Fusion Power even means. At best they think it is something to do with existing atomic-power stations, whereas in reality there is hardly any connection at all. Conventional nuclear generators use strongly-radioactive materials like uranium or plutonium that have large but unstable atoms that split into smaller pieces and release heat that is then used to run a steam turbine. However safe the newer designs of power plant are thought to be, concerns about transporting and storing nuclear waste, nuclear accidents and risks of terrorism are inherent in the technology. In contrast, a Fusion Power generator takes the smallest atoms and forces them together to create larger atoms along with the release of huge amounts of energy. It is the same process that powers the sun.

To make power commercially this way you need to force together atoms of two unusual forms ('isotopes') of hydrogen called Deuterium and Tritium to form helium. Normal hydrogen is the smallest atom in nature, just one positive proton and one negative electron. It is incredibly common. Deuterium is effectively hydrogen in which one neutron (a neutral sub-atomic particle) has been added. It is common in nature and is readily available from sea water. Tritium, in contrast, is hydrogen with two extra neutrons. Because it is very rare it will need to be specially manufactured for Fusion Power. But that is a relatively easy thing to do.

The good news is that the technique behind commercial Fusion Power combines readily-available or easily manufactured fuel with no greenhouse gas emissions, no possibility of a catastrophic accident, no weapons threat, safe decommissioning, low-level problems of waste management, and with the potential to satisfy almost unlimited power requirements safely for millions if not billions of years. That sort of power could, for example,

Fusion power

provide pervasive affordable water-desalination throughout the world. The bad news is that even after fifty years' research, developments are currently estimated as still about thirty years away from fully-commercial systems.

THE PHYSICS FORMULA THAT EVERYONE KNOWS

Fusion Power is what Einstein described with his famous $E=mc^2$. All his formula is saying is that if people want to know the maximum energy (E) they could get from nuclear fusion they just take the mass of the small amount of material that is in fact lost when atoms are fused (m) and multiply it by a fixed number – which might as well be called 'x'. The reason that instead of x it is written as c^2 is because this particular fixed number corresponds to a very big number indeed. It is the speed of light (conventionally written in physics equations as 'c') multiplied by itself. That is a very large number, which means that a Fusion Power generator – even if it is highly inefficient – need only use up a miniscule amount of raw material to create a tremendous amount of energy.

The reason why it now looks so likely that developers will definitely *reach* that goal though – is Simulation. The point is that it is incredibly difficult to work out how to build a mini-sun in a laboratory yet stop it burning a hole through the equipment. Nevertheless, recent advances have allowed exceptionally sophisticated simulations to be created and designs to be tested before building (typically extremely expensive) prototypes in the real world. That is now making a huge difference.

There are broadly two attractive routes to Fusion Power that governments are funding in a major way. The most popular uses powerful magnetic fields to keep the hugely hot reaction away from walls of a donut-shaped vessel. Technically this form of 'magnetic confinement fusion' is referred to as a *tokamak* reactor, which was a Russian acronym used by Soviet scientists to describe the original magnetic-donut design they devised in the 1950s. A leading example of this approach is the heavily-funded consortium of the European Union, India, Japan, the People's Republic of China, Russia, South Korea and the USA, called ITER (from 'International Thermonuclear Experimental Reactor'). This group currently anticipates a full-scale power plant by 2040.

SIMULATION

The second route to Fusion Power, adopted by the rival group HiPER, fires very-high-energy lasers at a stream of tiny pellets to set off a series of miniature explosions – up to ten each second – a bit like an automobile engine firing on different cylinders. The term 'HiPER' is actually a (not very good) acronym standing for HIgh Power laser Energy Research facility. The Europe-based project builds on the 'proof of principle' announced in 2010 by the National Ignition Facility in the USA. The potential attraction of this laser approach is that the reactor core is far more accessible because it is not enclosed by a huge magnet, so it should be easier to extract energy and perform maintenance. But whatever the relative attractions of the two main approaches, the important point is that both (as well as a few other research-lottery gambles) are being *seriously* funded.

Although Fusion Power is still a long way off, and although even the relatively few politicians that understand its potential are rightly playing it down, the fact remains that behind the scenes there is tremendous very-long-term international commitment to making it happen. Those critics that dismiss the likelihood of Fusion Power by 2040, underestimate the impact that the exponential growth of the Simulation trend will have on every aspect of development. They also miss the equally crucial role that breakthrough nanomaterials will have on reactor design. And they misread how deeply embedded the issue of energy-security has become to the civil servants around the world who, out of sight, and typically with much longer time-horizons than their political 'masters', carry far greater responsibility for deeply-complex scientific issues such as Fusion Power policy than the public ever realizes.

CHANGING WHAT IT MEANS TO BE ALIVE

Biotechnology is being transformed by the ability to use Simulation to decide how to refine the genetic code of organisms like bacteria so as to improve their properties

THE OTHER VITALLY important field in which Simulation is set to change people's lives also relates to modeling atoms, but in this case they are the atoms of complex carbon-based molecules. These are the types of molecules that build living organisms, and because their makeup and behavior tend to be far more difficult to understand than normal chemicals, until relatively recently it has only been their high-level impact that has been studied – and called 'Biology'. Now however, thanks to science's newfound ability to use computers to model the *detail* of what is actually going on, the field of Molecular Biology is taking off. It will impact everything from energy sources, waste recycling and pollution control to agriculture, fish-farming and forestry. And one of the main reasons that Simulation is set to provide such a massive boost to this aspect of the world economy is because of a fact that very few people tend to think about: Computers and Life encode information in very similar ways.

Although it is not often described in this way, the DNA in living cells is in reality a form of Digitization. Throughout the length of a DNA molecule, the two spirals of its famous 'double-helix' are held together by a vast number of minute chemical links (human DNA has about three billion). But there are just four types – any given link of any given DNA molecule is only ever one of those four types. Just as computer programs are encoded as a series of Ones and Zeros, so the building instructions for living organisms are encoded as a long sequence of only those four types of chemical link. A long-enough pattern of links to contain the instructions needed to reproduce a particular inheritable trait (such as an aspect of eye-color) is called a 'gene', and understanding how these patterns work is what genetics is all about.

The recent milestone in decoding the human genome (in other words listing the whole sequence of chemical links in human DNA) has resulted in computer-based DNA libraries that not only list the sequence of particular genes, but make those lists available free of charge to any researcher via the internet. More and more sequences are being added because, whereas it took about thirteen years to sequence one human genome in full, it now takes a week or so – and there are plans that within this decade it will take minutes and cost less than a meal at a nice restaurant.

DECODING GENOMES

The total sequence of chemical links in a given sample of deoxyribonucleic acid (DNA) is called the Genome. It corresponds to all the genes in the DNA as well as a tremendous number of what were originally thought to be redundant links that did not seem to serve any clear purpose, and so were called 'junk DNA'. These days, however, those unexplained links are thought to include sequences that have roles relating to functions such as how the DNA is copied. As a result, they are now referred to 'non-coding DNA'. In humans, all the separate genes (each of which impacts a particular inherited trait like eye-color) are clustered together into a total of forty-six 'chromosomes' arranged as twenty-three pairs – with the code of each half of a given chromosome-pair originally deriving from a different parent. Human eye color actually has rather complex genetics with various genes involved that are on different chromosomes. Despite what used to be thought, we now know that a baby's eyes can potentially be almost any color whatever the eye colors of its parents.

Thanks to the internet, poorly-funded researchers (even school children) now have access to the same unprecedented genetic data as the best-endowed institutions. It is this internet-enhanced form of research, often called 'bioinformatics', that is set to contribute to an extraordinary boost for molecular biology over the next few decades.

BIOTECH

The first impact to consider is Biotechnology. Although this risks becoming yet another overhyped umbrella-term, conceptually it is nothing more than the modern form of ancient technologies like brewing. Biotech finds practical applications for biology by using it to help make things just as Master Brewers use the fact that yeast ferments starch into alcohol to help them turn barley, water and hops into beer.

LATIN RESEARCH

Simulating biology experiments on a computer is often called *in silico* research – to distinguish it from what previously were the only two alternatives for biological research – *in vitro* (Latin for 'in glass', in other words something like a Petri dish or test tube) or *in vivo* (in a living organism).

Conceptually, Biotech is a more immediately-practical alternative to the largely-theoretical nanobots covered already in the chapter on Miniaturization. In essence it involves using, or even making, microscopic organisms that can manipulate atoms the ways the bioengineers want – which is what yeast fungus does to starch molecules. It is just that with Biotech, instead of building these 'devices' (as might be done with Nanotech) they are *grown*. And, because the biotech can be simulated on computer, bioengineers can first conduct large numbers of virtual experiments to see what will happen.

For several years already, biotech has produced safe forms of substances like insulin, human growth hormone and certain cancer treatments. Moving forward, biotech will be used to manufacture the new types of antibiotics needed to counter strongly-resistant strains of unpleasant things like gonorrhea and MRSA. It will also prove crucial in producing useful amounts of anti-viral vaccines as well as powerful drugs based around biological components that are otherwise extremely expensive, such as interferon. Other biotech substances will clean up environments contaminated by pollution in a similar way to how microbes on the forest floor rot fallen trees down into nutritious components. This is already developing into the commercial field of Bioremediation.

SIMULATION

GENETIC ENGINEERING AND SYNTHETIC BIOLOGY

The main reason why biotech is fast accelerating into all these new territories is that researchers are now deliberately refining the genetic code of biological organisms to change certain characteristics. For instance, yeast has been modified to convert sugar not into alcohol but into diesel fuel. At the forefront of such research is the rapidly emerging field of Synthetic Biology. In 2010 scientists for the first time made a *synthetic* genome for bacteria. They decoded the genome of a strain of naturally occurring bacteria, stored the genome as computer software, used that software to synthesize DNA just like the original, and then inserted that synthesized DNA into a recipient cell that dutifully turned itself into the 'new' species that the code specified (namely the original bacteria whose genome had been decoded and stored as computer-bits).

That cell then successfully replicated more than a billion times, resulting in the slightly overblown claim that scientists had created artificial life. To be precise, although the scientists created what they called a 'synthetic cell' it was only the genome itself that was truly synthetic, and even that was a computer-synthesized copy of a naturally-occurring original. More accurately, therefore, the scientists had *recreated* life. Nevertheless, it is indisputable that the bacteria's direct parent was a computer – not anything living – which is quite remarkable.

Mainstream research uses building blocks taken from naturally-occurring genomes. Scientists remove a carefully-selected sequence from one string of DNA, extract a sequence from another type of DNA (maybe even from another species entirely), and then recombine the two sequences into one new string of DNA that typically could never occur in nature. Technically this is referred to a Recombinant DNA (or rDNA) technology, and when the inserted sequence is from a different species the end-result becomes what is called a 'transgenic' organism. On first consideration that seems a highly radical or even dangerous thing to do. And, by definition, it is certainly not 'natural'. In the next subchapter I will explain the way that the risks and ethics of this sort of work are playing out. But it is important first to understand why the instinctive concerns many people feel do not necessarily correspond to how Nature itself actually seems to work.

Despite the way most people interpret Darwin, in truth, biological evolution and 'survival of the fittest' is far more about Genes than it is even about Cells, let alone Animals. The ultimate units of biological information, the most-important building blocks of nature, are in reality genes, not the enormous DNA molecules in which the genes reside. Science now understands that in many ways a DNA molecule as a whole is nothing more than a huge filing cabinet that acts like a historical archive reflecting all the environmental changes that took place in the past, and all the different genes that played a part (many of them common to other species), as well as a whole load of replication instructions together with apparently redundant information that no longer serves much if any purpose.

Once Genetic Engineering is viewed in this light, it is far less relevant whether a gene comes from a totally different species, because across billions of years that is exactly what nearly all genes have done. In many ways it is misleading to talk about 'inserting an animal gene into plant DNA' because the gene itself does not *belong* to either, any more than a file containing domestic-electricity bills 'belongs' to an Accounting filing cabinet rather than a Home filing cabinet. Its original location is simply where it is found, and if it is an active file then it clearly works reasonably well within that particular filing system. But it may work in another system as well.

In terms of Information, artificially inserting a gene from another species is just a form of Networking. It is a mechanism for sharing what effectively is digitized biological software between two or more different systems. Indeed, workers within the field of synthetic biology already think of strands of DNA merely as components with which to build 'biocircuits' that can potentially be designed to do anything, even interact directly with computer circuitry. But of course, as is well known from the internet, some software is dangerous to share between computers. Sometimes, even if a program works well on one system, it can corrupt another. Biological software is no different. When it comes to sharing genetic information, what is crucial – and what will dramatically impact the future of genetic engineering and synthetic biology – is whether the end result is considered *safe*. That is what we will consider next.

Reaping the whirlwind of GM-crops

Genetically-Modified crops offer extraordinary benefits and most (though not all) concerns are overblown – but GM-crop take-up will still be driven by lobbying not science

LET US START with why all this matters at all. If only the international community can avoid any of the inherent risks perceived to be associated with something like genetically modified (GM) plants, then the benefits are potentially extraordinary. Agricultural crop yields can be improved, plants can be made less vulnerable to environmental stresses like droughts or salt, they can be made more nutritious or contain more vitamins, made to taste better, have a better texture, store better after they have been harvested, and even made more digestible (for humans or livestock).

In addition, crops can be made less dependent on chemical fertilizers and pesticides, they can be made toxic to the insects that attack them, or resistant to the herbicides used to control the weeds that otherwise would strangle them, they can be made more resistant to microbial diseases like fungus or bacteria, they can be made to smell better, look prettier, have different colored flowers or leaves or fruit, have a better shape, grow taller or shorter, straighter or broader, and they can even be made to produce incredibly useful medicines like insulin, or even edible vaccines that can simply be swallowed rather than injected (up until now simple chemicals like vitamins have tended to be given orally whereas the large molecules in vaccines have required injection).

The point is that modern research is coming up with potentially life-changing products that, if only they truly are safe, will make a major difference to issues like world hunger and balanced nutrition; some 'potentially unsafe' GM-crop developments are not just nice to have but they can reduce substantial suffering. They can save lives. For example, vitamin deficiency is a problem for millions of people. As a result of lack of

Vitamin A, hundreds of thousands of children each year go blind and are also far less able to fight off disease. Several years ago, a strain of GM rice fortified with Vitamin A was developed that may help, not least because a deal was struck to make it affordable in developing countries by waiving royalty payments for the large number of patents involved in its production.

GOLDEN RICE

Commonly known as 'Golden Rice', a special strain of genetically-modified rice contains artificially high levels of beta-carotene (an excellent source of Vitamin A). Getting the royalty payments waived was only the first barrier to its adoption in poor countries that suffer from widespread Vitamin-A deficiency. Next came strong but well-intentioned opposition from anti-GM campaigners. Whatever the rights or wrongs of the process, throughout the delays, a million or more children nevertheless went blind from lack of Vitamin A. Statistically about half of them will have died soon after.

But, despite strong support from large numbers of scientific experts, it nevertheless came up against strong anti-GM lobbying that for a long while blocked its adoption. This sort of dynamic is very different to what is happening in the Digitization, Networking and Miniaturization trends, or indeed in many other parts of the Simulation trend. The future impact of GM crops is far more to do with the success of different groups in swaying public opinion than it is to do with pure costs and benefits. As a result, many economists struggle to understand how this aspect of the global economy will develop. But it is actually a lot clearer than it seems.

WORRIES OVER GM CROPS

The main concerns about GM crops are of five types: GM crops might be dangerous to eat; interbreeding with non-GM plants could result in, for example, pesticide-resistance being transferred to weeds; killing agricultural pests could impact other more beneficial insects and animals that depend on them; multinational producers of patented GM crops and associated chemicals could easily hold farmers, and indeed whole countries, to ransom; and finally, high-productivity GM crops might not be affordable to the poorest nations, which therefore would unfairly be placed at a disadvantage and sink still further into poverty.

These are five very different types of worry, ranging from purely-scientific issues about food-safety all the way to ethical issues about the obligations of rich nations. But they are usually all lumped together into simplistic questions like: 'Do you support GM crops?' As a result, the next thirty years of GM developments will primarily be dominated by beliefs, not scientific data. Indeed, the same data will be interpreted *differently* depending on what people's wider beliefs are. For instance, the general public in Europe and Japan has on balance strongly opposed GM crops, even when that has not reflected the views of their own scientific communities (and, ironically, even though nearly all the huge volume of cheese that these countries produce and eat is made using a genetically-engineered enzyme).

A CHEESY STORY

Just as catalysts change the speed of chemical reactions, enzymes do the same for biological reactions – so effectively enzymes are just biological catalysts. In cheese making, rennet contains the enzyme that is added to acidified milk to separate it into solid curds and liquid whey. Until recently it came from the lining of a cow's fourth stomach. These days nearly all cheese producers prefer to use a genetically-engineered form of rennet. And most consumers – even those strongly opposed to genetic engineering – are unaware of the fact.

Meanwhile, over the last fifteen years in the USA, hundreds of millions of people have been eating GM foods without any apparent ill-effects. And even the strictly religious and rigorously traditional Amish community (which avoids modern technology and still ploughs fields using horse-drawn tractors) has nevertheless adopted GM crops. Yet the European, Japanese and American public all potentially have access to the same data. How can they interpret it so differently?

What is happening is that they are drawing different conclusions because the concerted efforts of governments, industries, academia and environmental groups operate very differently in the three locations. And some of those dynamics are deeply cultural and are not set to change over the next few decades. The same is true all around the world. The implication is that, unless a *major* danger is found that is demonstrated beyond doubt and that applies across all GM crops, the pattern that has already formed is largely set to continue.

Relatively rich communities like Europe and Japan will initially find it easy to maintain the luxury of sticking to the Precautionary Principle that until GM crops can be proved to be completely safe then it is better to avoid them. Given that many of the five different concerns have some very-long-term components, it is in practice almost impossible for advocates of GM crops to satisfy such a high burden of proof in less than several decades. What is more, new generations of GM plants are being released elsewhere, which effectively sets the clock back to the beginning – just because first-generation crops were safe does not automatically imply that subsequent developments will be.

With that said, on the assumption that the global public sees few negative consequences in large-scale 'test sites' such as the USA, and as European and Japanese farmers increasingly feel at a disadvantage – heightened by the current global economic downturn – there is likely to be a gradual softening of attitude. At that point, there will be renewed attempts by scientists and pharmaceutical companies and (initially only a few) politicians to 'enroll the public'. Only as those efforts begin to show promise will governments risk changes in legislation. Poorer countries, as well as richer countries like China and India that nevertheless have very poor rural populations, have much less choice in holding to the Precautionary Principle. They will tend increasingly-enthusiastically to press ahead with GM crops.

The wheat genome is five times larger than the human genome and has a far more complex structure. Nevertheless, with draft sequences of the very-complex wheat genome already completed in 2010, developments began accelerating faster than ever. As a result, and despite all the current rhetoric, GM crops are set to take hold, and hopefully ease a lot of suffering in the process. Indeed, that is likely to remain true even if some concerns *do* eventually turn out to be justified. Based on everything that I am aware of that is going on behind the scenes, my conclusion is that *most* of the GM concerns will slowly evaporate. Determining food safety is a well-established process and it is relatively easy for governments to ensure that GM crops are at least as safe as other foods. Very-long-term effects are far harder to test for, but the same is true for sugary drinks, salty chips, high-fat burgers and alcohol – and strong medical evidence against having too much of those has had little impact in many developed countries.

Interbreeding between plants is theoretically possible though for various reasons is thought likely to be rare. Even if it occurs it will be little different to the long-continued emergence of antibiotic-resistant strains of bacteria, and typically a lot less dangerous. Concerns about exploitation by 'greedy globalized multinationals' can if necessary be addressed by regulation. And, risks of widening the divide between rich and poor nations raises a problem that is far broader than just GM crops. Ultimately, it is a political issue that is only open to a political solution.

However, there is one of the concerns about GM crops that is not so easily downplayed: The worry that a GM crop, although 'safe' in its own right, might nevertheless result in major unintended consequences is a very genuine issue. As an example, an apparently benign GM plant that has been made toxic to certain pests may as a result deprive insects that usually eat those pests of an important food source and starve them to death. Those insects might have been important pollinators for agricultural crops. Or they might have also preyed on other pests that, now their predator is gone, explode in number. Maybe one of those plagues of pests carries a disease that affects humans, causing an epidemic.

The point is that it is possible to make up almost any scary scenario. Far worse, it is impossible to guess what *all* those scenarios might be, let alone decide if any of them is more than just alarmist fiction. As highlighted in the final chapter of this book, these sorts of hidden and complex side-effects are extremely difficult to anticipate or manage. If GM-crop development hides any nasty surprises over the next several decades, they are most likely to be of this form.

ANIMAL CLONING WHEN THE ANIMAL HAPPENS TO BE HUMAN

Animal Cloning is another emotive topic that is clouded by 'ethics experts' who can be biased by religious beliefs – but artificial human-cloning *will* eventually happen

SIMULATING 'LIFE SCIENCES' – all the fields of study that relate to living organisms – is set truly to revolutionize medicine and veterinary science. Already, molecular biology dominates medical research, and it is genetic engineering that will be at the forefront. Scientists have already succeeded in genetically engineering malaria-resistant mosquitos and silk worms that spin strands containing much stronger spider-silk. Milk-producing animals can be used to manufacture special drugs or other substances in their milk – for instance, goats (just like silk worms) have been genetically modified to manufacture spider-silk. Pigs, which have similar insides to us, may be modified so organ transplants into human patients will not be rejected.

SPIDER GOATS

The dragline of silk that spiders use to catch themselves when they fall is an amazing substance – far stronger for its weight than high-tensile steel or even the Kevlar woven into bullet-proof jackets. Readily available spider-silk would open up a huge range of opportunities. But chemists cannot make it. And spiders are so cannibalistic that they cannot be farmed. However, the spider-silk gene has successfully been introduced into goat DNA in such a way that the otherwise-normal goat milk contains an extra protein, the same protein that a spider uses to form silk. The milk is filtered to remove fats and then a thread of silk is slowly drawn from the purified liquid-proteins that remain.

SIMULATION

Already today, genetically-modified hormones are given to a wide range of farm animals in some countries. However, it is in the field of Cloning – producing genetically identical copies of an organism – that some of the most important, and contentious, developments will occur. When it comes to horticulture, no one seems to have any problems with cloning. When someone plants a potato and it grows into a crop, they are all clones. Certain particularly valuable types of grape-vine have been cloned down the centuries from an original parent that grew a couple of thousand years ago. No one proposes regulating this sort of cloning.

MODIFIED GROWTH HORMONES IN DAIRY CATTLE

Bovine somatotropin (BST) is a growth hormone in cattle. Using recombinant DNA technology, a genetically-engineered form of BST (known as rBST) has been manufactured and widely used in the USA since the mid-'90s to boost milk production in dairy cows. This has certainly raised concerns, but reported health issues – such as mastitis and joint problems – may be a problem of using growth hormones at all rather than of using a *genetically-engineered* growth hormone. Either way, in the USA, milk produced using rBST does not require special labeling. In contrast, throughout Australia, Canada, Europe, Japan and New Zealand it is banned.

Moreover, despite the way most people talk about the subject, and despite heavy regulation, there are *already* human clones. Many of them. That is because what we call 'identical twins' are actually nothing more nor less than clones. But because they occur naturally, no one seems bothered. It is when it comes to *artificial* cloning of animals and humans that people tend suddenly to take a very different view. Consequently, as with GM crops, the default future of cloning is determined less by scientific breakthrough, economic strength or environmental pressure and more by deep-seated bias.

The official line by governments around the world goes something like this: Subject to the case-by-case decisions of Ethics Experts, when it comes to humans then 'therapeutic cloning' (that is, cloning cells for medical research) is generally OK, but 'reproductive cloning' (of a whole human being) is completely unacceptable and will forever be banned. However, the apparent meaning of this official position is completely misleading. And the suggestion that there will not be artificial human-cloning within the next few decades is almost certainly wrong.

Starting with the misleading aspects of this supposed global policy: To most people, including many politicians, it seems very reasonable that the ethical minefield of 'tampering with Nature' should ultimately be policed by recognized experts in ethics. If they are Professors or on some official Committee then all the better. The problem is that Ethics – seeking answers to moral questions – is not a rigorous science that is easily raised above personal prejudice. What is more, in my experience, the quality of 'experts' in the field is extremely variable. Nor is high position an automatic indicator of impartiality. As a result, national interpretations of the 'official line' on cloning vary enormously around the world, not least because, as we will now examine, those interpretations are heavily influenced by religion.

RELIGION AND HUMAN CLONING

Based on their claim that life begins at conception, the Roman Catholic Church tends to be against all forms of cloning. Judaism in contrast does not appear to have such a fundamental objection. Buddhists believing in the recycling of life can justify cloning embryos, as do some Hindus. Confucians do not equate an embryo with a person, so nations such as China (which is officially atheist anyway) can approach the whole minefield from an utterly different perspective, as can increasingly secular countries such as the UK, Netherlands and Scandinavia. Meanwhile, countries like the USA that theoretically separate Church and State can nevertheless have federal policy heavily influenced by the religious beliefs of the Ethics Experts advising the President.

Ultimately, all the 'ethical decisions' being made worldwide are often totally dependent upon whether those making the ruling believe that, for instance, a ball of all-purpose cells smaller than the head of a pin has the same rights and deserves the same protection as a ten-year-old child in pain or an eighty-year-old adult with dementia. In practice, it is impossible for compassionate human beings to make that sort of judgment in isolation of their religion or atheism and of their overall world view. And *that* context utterly changes depending on who is making the decision.

SIMULATION

As a result, despite the worldwide ban, artificial human-cloning is set to happen. The main reason why at the moment all countries are agreed it is a bad idea is not, as some strident voices suggest, because they all agree that it is 'playing God' or that 'trying to improve on Nature will ultimately lead to a form of genocide in which ordinary humans die out' or 'we should not interfere with Life'. The reason why no one can condone the research is that it is currently very dangerous. Science does not yet know how to clone a whole animal without causing complications that lead to early death, as happened with Dolly the sheep. That is bad enough when the process creates a damaged animal. It is unthinkably cruel to take the same risk with a human baby.

But the time will come when sufficient successful experiments have been run with animals that, despite any remaining ban, some researcher somewhere will illicitly clone a human being. If I had to guess, it will be in Asia. Within a few decades from now, richer people will be able to seek help in creating a clone, maybe even at low risk to all concerned. On first consideration that may seem to be a supremely arrogant and selfish action for those involved to take. But their motives may not be so clear-cut. Parents could seek a clone, for instance, to provide a life-saving transplant for their otherwise-dying child. Making such a decision would still be an ethical minefield, but their desperation for a clone might well be driven by love rather than egotism.

Those wanting a human clone will quite likely have to travel, because the national bans in some countries may remain for as long as the dominance of their national religion. But without a DNA test it will be impossible for anyone to prove that the resultant baby is a clone. Even with a DNA test, it would be very hard to prove beyond all doubt that someone did not simply freeze the embryo of an identical twin for birth at a later date. And anyway, under an appeal to basic human rights, it is very difficult to imagine what legal footing any government would be able to sustain for legislating against one form of identical-twin over another.

THE JURASSIC-PARK QUESTION

It is very likely that previously-extinct species – even woolly mammoths – will be brought back from extinction (although dinosaur DNA appears to be far too degraded)

THIS IS THE classic Jurassic Park question: Within the next few decades, will the first ever extinct species be bought back to life as a result of cloning DNA from preserved tissue? The simple answer is No. But that is only because very few people realize that the first extinct species has *already* been bought back – albeit fleetingly. The very last Pyrenean Ibex, a female called Celia, was found dead on January 6th 2000. However, a year before, a tissue sample had been taken from her and preserved. After several attempts, in 2009 a female Ibex cloned from cells of the sample taken a decade earlier was born alive, although it only survived seven minutes before then dying of breathing difficulties.

Nevertheless, it is an impressive start. Within only a few years expect to hear about a string of successes. As far as longer-term headline-grabbing possibilities are concerned, look out for the possible return of the Tasmanian Tiger that went extinct seventy-five years ago. Correctly named a Thylacine, it was a dog-like shape with rather attractive stripes – certainly photogenic enough for major media attention. The last known specimen died in 1936. Its return from extinction would represent a major milestone because it would involve successfully patching together the full genetic code from a series of badly contaminated museum samples.

No one should hold their breath for the reintroduction of dinosaurs. Despite the claims that 'it would be wrong to bring them back into a totally different ecosystem', of course people will nevertheless try. But it is an immensely difficult challenge to piece together enough DNA. However, by 2040 the world may well have something almost as impressive – woolly mammoths. A few frozen specimens, preserved for tens of thousands of years in permafrost, have been found to contain DNA that is in far better condition than was originally assumed. And DNA taken from inside hairs, for instance, tends to be much less contaminated.

SIMULATION

LONG-EXTINCT DNA FROM EGGSHELLS

The most suitable source of potentially-retrievable DNA from long-extinct animals may be eggs preserved in permafrost. Eggshells break down very slowly – which is why they often remain in compost heaps. However, although some DNA has recently been extracted from ancient eggshells, the oldest (an emu egg in Australia) was still only 19,000 years old. Even though dinosaurs did indeed produce eggs, the most recent examples were laid just before the dinos died out. And that was 65-*million* years ago.

What is more, there are sufficient similarities to the genome of modern-day African elephants that it might be possible to 'fill-in' any gaps in the mammoth-sequences. It will take a lot of time, and some suggest that it is wasted money. But these detractors perhaps underestimate the power of symbolism. Modern humans are, quite rightly, increasingly seeing themselves as destroyers of the environment, polluters of the planet, and the direct cause of much extinction. It is not a very uplifting self-image. Just for once, in addition to any scientific benefits it achieved, it might just feel good simply to bring something back.

WHY SUPERMAN FOUGHT FOR STEM-CELL RESEARCH

Stem Cell research offers the potential of life-changing therapies for everything from Alzheimer's and strokes to the replacement of detective organs such as hearts

ONE OF THE greatest frustrations of 'Superman' Christopher Reeve, after a riding accident broke his spinal cord and made him a quadriplegic, was the set of regulatory restrictions on stem-cell research in the USA. In 2001, President George W Bush introduced an official block on federally-funded research. Despite his almost-complete paralysis, Christopher Reeve lobbied tirelessly against this, right up until his death in 2004. The following year, against strong advice, President Bush used his personal veto once again to block attempts to promote stem-cell research. As a direct result, leftover embryos from *in vitro* infertility treatments (a standard source of stem cells for research) had to be destroyed rather than used to seek ways to reduce the all-too-real suffering of the living. Only upon the election of President Barack Obama were the restrictions rapidly repealed.

Cloning 'stem cells' – special general-purpose cells that can transform into any of the more-specialized cells like muscle or bone or brain – offers the chance of repairing not just spinal-cord injuries but also heart damage, brain deterioration (from things like strokes, Parkinson's and Alzheimer's), treating cancers such as leukemia, curing deafness and blindness, diabetes, and some forms of infertility. Eventually, though it is surprisingly more difficult than originally thought, there should even be stem-cell therapies for baldness. All these treatments now seem likely to become available over the next two decades.

In addition, we should begin to see therapeutic cloning from stem cells of whole organs such as kidneys, livers and even hearts that can be transplanted into patients without risk of rejection. Already, various clinical trials have successfully used heart-attack patients' own stem cells to regenerate parts of their damaged hearts, reducing the non-beating scar tissue caused by cardiac arrest while simultaneously stimulating regrowth of healthy heart-muscle. Far more radically, in the research lab it has proved possible to wash a donor heart with detergent for three days to lose all its cells and just leave the scaffolding that previously held the cells in the right structure, a so-called 'ghost heart'. That can then be repopulated with stem cells (taken and then cloned in order to get sufficient numbers) from a patient with a damaged heart. Researchers are close to growing a fully-functioning new heart that, with further work, could potentially be transplanted into a patient and started with an electrical stimulus.

Soon, therapeutic cloning techniques will have superseded even today's already-amazing approaches. And the trend is now unstoppable, even though recent examples of complications suggest that many of the problems to be overcome in stem-cell therapy have not yet even been recognized, let alone understood. Whatever the (sometimes religiously-inspired) restrictions imposed in some countries, across many parts of the world researchers into stem-cell therapies have forged ahead and as a result are already relieving immense suffering and anguish that otherwise would have remained. However strident the opposition of a few powerful conservative factions, the international community of stem-cell researchers is not now going to capitulate. If necessary, the best medical scientists will simply move to more supportive environments, and the obstructive economies they leave will increasingly lose out as a result. The existing breakthroughs in stem-cell therapy are only just the beginning.

GENE THERAPY AND A BRAVER NEW WORLD

Genetic Therapies can reflect the unique details of an individual's DNA so as to screen for diseases, customize treatments, and potentially change unwanted genes

IT IS EASY to come up with numerous examples of how the High-Tech supertrend as a whole will change humanity. But it is only really the impacts that the *Simulation* trend will make that are set to change people from the inside out. That is because molecular biology is on course to alter not just how medicine views disease, but even what conditions are considered to need treating as if they were a disease – 'old age' for instance. All this is being made possible by Simulation helping researchers understand how cells work. And it is becoming such an extremely productive field because simulating in ever-greater detail how cells operate, particularly focusing on the role of DNA, offers extraordinary opportunities.

It turns out, for example, that drugs behave differently depending on the details of one person's DNA compared with another. So by decoding a patient's DNA and then simulating how different variations of drug will react, it will be possible to tailor therapies to have maximum positive effect yet do minimum damage to healthy cells. In addition, because different people process given drugs at different rates, it will also be possible to ensure that a particular patient receives exactly the right dose *for them*, and so minimizes any unavoidable side-effects. Already this type of research into the influence of genetic variations on drug therapy has expanded into a new field of study called 'pharmacogenomics'.

This kind of personalized medicine is possible only because of the ability to model the behavior of individual genes. But that ability opens up many additional opportunities as well. Therapies can be tightly targeted at specific genes and proteins that cause disease. Vaccines can be customized that protect against several strains of disease at once without any risk of infection. And maybe most intriguing, and certainly most provocative, defective genes can be replaced. This sort of 'gene therapy' comes in many forms. Current research focuses on making changes that cannot be passed onto future generations; more technically, the genetic changes are made to 'somatic' cells but not to 'germ' cells (that is, sperm or eggs that contain DNA that can be transferred to offspring).

Nevertheless, even somatic-gene therapy is fraught with technical and ethical difficulties. Somehow the therapy must affect all of the defective genes relating to a hereditary disease like muscular dystrophy, yet avoid affecting healthy cells or setting off an allergic reaction. That is difficult enough. However, it turns out there are very few genetic disorders (whether they are hereditary or, like many cancers, resulting from mutation) that are caused by only one defective gene. In practice, it is often very difficult to work out how to use gene therapy because most genetic diseases involve *many* genes.

HOW MANY GENES DO YOU HAVE?

The answer is: Very much fewer than geneticists until recently assumed. It turns out that roughly only 23,000 genes contain all the coding for the protein building-blocks that are used to create a human. Yet between them all those genes represent only about 1.5% of the overall human-genome – very much less than experts supposed even a few years ago.

The Human Genome Project revealed the big surprise that each individual has far fewer genes than was expected to build a complete human, only about twenty-three thousand. That makes it perfectly clear that the genetic manual is far more sophisticated than just a one-to-one mapping of single (or even multiple) genes to individual human traits. Other factors must play an important role too. It is now known that in many cases a cell's environment affects when and in what way a particular gene acts. That is a crucial discovery because it means that all of the predictions people have been making up to now about 'designer children' and 'cures for all genetic disorders' being just around the corner – are completely wrong. In reality, simulating how genes affect someone is far more complex than just modeling the molecules of their DNA. Instead it requires taking account of the whole *system* in which those molecules fit. And that is a major reason why the Simulation trend will remain so crucial over the next thirty years.

ETHICS OF GENE THERAPY

Throughout that period, Simulation will drive astonishing developments in genetics. As already covered on page 110, the first are likely to relate to genetic testing for predisposition to specific diseases. But this does raise several ethical considerations. For a start, how valid is it for Health Insurance companies to require full-disclosure of someone's DNA? And what about tests for currently-incurable diseases? On balance, for example, is it helpful for a young vibrant person to be told that they have Huntington's disease and as a result by middle-age are expected slowly to lose all physical coordination and mentally deteriorate into dementia? And if a mother chooses to abort a pregnancy because of a genetic defect, who gets to decide what constitutes a 'defect' and what is merely a trait that the mother does not want in her offspring, given that in some cultures that 'undesirable trait' might simply be being the wrong gender?

In that context, though, it is worth remembering that for millions of years humans have informally been selecting traits for their offspring merely by choosing with whom they reproduce. Although formal selective-breeding in humans, 'eugenics', is deeply tainted by its enthusiastic adoption by the Nazis, its animal-breeding equivalent has given us everything from toy-poodles to low-fat dairy herds. Most modern genetic-therapists understandably try to avoid association with the field of eugenics, but the reality is that the future of their field very much overlaps that territory.

Certainly, today many parents of all backgrounds go to immense trouble to 'fine tune' their children, not least by selecting the ways that they are educated and the diet they eat. The claims of some ethicists that genetic therapies affecting babies (whether directly or by inheriting genetic changes made to a parent) are unacceptable breaches of a baby's rights, are in many ways now irrelevant given how this trend has already formed. Genetic 'improvements' to humans will eventually happen anyway. And they will usually happen for the best of parental intentions. Most parents will happily 'interfere with the rights of an unborn child' if it means their baby is born without a genetic disease. In due course, if safe genetic therapy can improve the odds that their child may grow up stronger or faster or smarter or simply healthier, some parents will consider that paying for the treatment, and travelling to wherever they have to go to get it, represents a gift to their child of the best start in life they can provide – even though they realize that environmental factors will still play a major role in deciding the eventual outcome. What is more, genetic therapies will not just be reserved for the next generation. Many of the current generation will want them for themselves. And that is set to change the fate of some people alive today.

WHY TOMORROW'S 150-YEAR-OLDS MAY BE IN THEIR 50S TODAY

The economics of the pharmaceutical industry mean anti-aging therapies are set dramatically to extend lifespans – some 50-year-olds today may live to 150 (or far more)

THERE IS ONE aspect of the Simulation trend that is far more deeply established than most of the general public realizes, far more focused on rich nations than many humanitarians would wish, and far more radical than some religious leaders can accept: Extended Life. The reason why this aspect of our future is already largely unstoppable is not just that throughout history (despite the promise of various competing afterlives) a surprising number of people have nevertheless wanted to stay as long as possible in *this* life. The main reason why dramatically-increased longevity is now locked into the default future – is the economics of the pharmaceutical industry.

Regulation of drugs and medical treatments is very tight. The general public, quite rightly, wants it to be. As a result, it costs a staggering amount to develop a new drug, test it, demonstrate that it is safe, and get it licensed. Those very few drugs that make it all the way through that process have to carry the costs of all the experiments that failed. As a result, these days it often costs around a *billion dollars* to bring a completely new type of therapy to market. That new therapy then needs to sell enough before its patents run out to pay back the pharmaceutical company, invest in new research, and make a profit. All this means that there are many worthwhile drugs that do not get to market because the approval costs cannot be financially justified, sometimes because an illness is too rare for enough people to buy a drug to treat it, and sometimes because the illness is only common in countries that are too poor to pay for treatment.

SIMULATION

Although these days many developed nations have policies designed to encourage pharmaceutical companies nevertheless to develop such 'orphan drugs', the overall bias still remains. In general, most of the time, the main focus of pharmaceutical research is on satisfying the needs of large and rich markets. Given the demographic bubbles highlighted later on page 189, the market in developed nations for anti-aging therapies is about as big and lucrative as it comes. In hugely-funded rival research labs around the world, some of the brightest pharmaceutical brains on the planet are racing toward the goal of combating aging.

It is an immensely complex subject that simply could not be tackled without the combined onslaught of Digitization providing the robotic labs used to conduct huge numbers of tests in parallel, Networking providing the supercomputers and internet-databases on which the research draws, Miniaturization providing the tools to intervene at the cellular level, and Simulation providing the ability to model the behavior of complex molecules. It is a consequence of the High-Tech launch engine operating at full throttle. And its eventual impact is likely to be extraordinary. In the last few years there have been many enthusiastic articles in the popular press wondering if current research means there will soon be 150-year-olds. Several scientists have consistently replied that the answer is No. They are quite correct. That is because they are being asked the wrong question. The real issue is whether there will be any 150-year-olds in another hundred years' time. That would mean those people were only about 50 today. The answer to *that* unasked question is: Quite possibly.

The logic goes like this. If someone can remain healthy until around 2040 then the benefits of on-going pharmaceutical and medical research into areas such as therapeutic cloning, stem-cells and genetic testing will increase their odds of remaining healthy for another ten years. By that stage there are very likely to be the first medical-research artificial intelligences funded by pharmaceutical companies. Quantum Computers will allow otherwise undiscoverable correlations to be mined from the wealth of clinical data stored on the supernet. And complex nanodrugs will either turn many killer-diseases (such as any remaining forms of cancer) into manageable conditions or will cure them entirely.

Then things will really take off. And yet those who were in their fifties when this book was first published will still only be in their nineties. Some of them may still happily be working because they will be far fitter and healthier than most ninety-year-olds were at the turn of the century, and

Global Renaissance

they will still be nowhere near breaking any records for longevity. As the accumulated knowledge on the supernet fuels the emergence of a more fundamental understanding of human physiology, individuals will be able to link themselves up to it full-time with, for instance, hundreds of miniaturized sensors. It will be like being in an intensive-care unit every second of the day and night. That should give at least a few people another ten years, provided they can either afford all the treatments and technology or get into the right research program at the right time.

And so, step by step, year by year, a diminishing number of individuals will gradually pull their longevity up by its own bootstraps. If they live in a country that is wealthy enough then sufficient of them will remain healthy enough that some of them survive to the next round. And the longer they survive, the better the technology becomes to help them make it to their 150th Birthday. Then the rejuvenation drugs will kick in. And then, at last, those long-awaited nanobots will finally become available that can float around in your bloodstream, monitoring and repairing anything that your body's own defenses miss. The sophisticated intelligence-amplifier you are connected to will mean you even understand how all your healthcare-technology works – and how, from its shaky start at the beginning of the 21st century, the international community pulled itself up into a Global Renaissance.

THE HIGH-TECH ROUTE TO GLOBAL RENAISSANCE

If we can avoid the worst counter-currents to the High-Tech supertrend – some caused by its own side-effects – its impacts will overall be positive and life-affirming

ONCE THE LOGIC behind dramatically-extended lifespan is analyzed, it does indeed seem quite probable that the overall High-Tech trajectory will lead to substantially longer lives for at least a few people already alive today. But that is just one of an extraordinary spectrum of changes that exponential High-Tech will bring. And many parts of the future only thirty years out are very much more likely even than developments such as substantial life-extension. The main features of the next several decades are created by trends that are now so deeply embedded into how 21st-century society operates that the only way they will go away is if society itself fundamentally breaks down, as touched on in the final chapter of this book. Excluding that possibility, it is already reasonably clear where the combined pressures of the four components of the High-Tech engine are set to take the international community.

By 2040, it is an unfamiliar future of huge megacities that sound completely alien because the electric-traffic noise (including the synthesized sounds generated to warn pedestrians that automobiles are close) is utterly different. Garage mechanics know about robotics but do not understand gear boxes. Children go to school to keep them safe during the day, but they mainly learn from the supernet. Huge TV screens on the sides of buildings promote sexy pop stars who only exist in cyberspace. And everywhere individuals go, systems monitor their whereabouts and advertise to them what they may be interested in – unless they switch their mobile to one of their fake persona. It is a strange future.

But it is also a future where people need never be lonely, never be bored. Their virtual assistant knows their moods better than they do. Individuals immerse themselves into the supernet and enjoy a party with friends they have not physically been able to travel to see for years. Later, they virtually pop to see how amazingly well their parents are doing now that the Alzheimer's has completely cleared up. And they are shown the new trick that the family robot-pet has just learned. Their mobile clicks up the News Release that the series of desalination plants powered by the first commercial-prototype Fusion generator have started irrigating a desert area the size of a small country. And on their 3-D wall panel they watch the release back into the wild of a pair of Tasmanian Tigers, just over a hundred years after the last one of the species became extinct.

Our future, thirty years out, is certainly no Utopia. But equally certainly, it is at last a time of great hope for all humanity, wherever we live, whatever our background. Ultimately, it is a future to be deeply proud of because, despite all the mistakes of the past, despite all its remaining faults, it has almost unlimited potential. And in that sense, it mirrors the very best of what it means to be human.

HOWEVER, as we will now explore in the final chapter, there are no guarantees. We are committed to sustaining the launch of our world economy. But nevertheless, our High-Tech engine is stirring up so much turbulence that we are increasingly at risk of being flung off course. The faster we go, the greater that self-induced threat. And yet if we fail to reach some form of Global Renaissance within around thirty years, then the instability that our progress has already triggered is likely to have escalated to such a degree as to have thrown us into progressive Global Chaos. We clearly have to do what we can to stabilize our trajectory, but there is not in practice very much time before it would simply take too much effort to make enough of a difference. We will likely have at least the next ten years to get serious about realigning our global society. But probably not fifteen.

Far be it from me, at this late stage, to start seeming melodramatic. In reality I think that our global society has a good chance. But we – and that really does include you – need to encourage some important changes pretty quickly. Suffice to say, if we were all characters within the script of a Hollywood blockbuster, this is the transition-point three-quarters way through the screenplay when one of the leading protagonists breaks the feel-good mood of the romantic sub-plot with something like: 'I love you, but we only have fourteen years to save the Earth!'

CHAPTER SUMMARY
SIMULATION

Simulation will support fundamental and sweeping advances that lead to almost limitless electricity and maybe almost limitless life-extension

Modeling the world with Simulation is the best way of transforming cutting-edge science into radical technology and life-changing medicine
- *Although it is now underpinned by the other three High-Tech trends, Simulation is an ancient trend deeply embedded into the global economy and is largely unstoppable*
- *Advances driven by Simulation will revolutionize almost every aspect of society – although the most far-reaching impacts will be to Fusion Power and Molecular Biology*

Fusion Power has an extraordinary potential to solve future energy demands but the chances of it being ready in time depend on Simulation
- *Despite strong pressures for economies to move away from oil-dependency, even a balance of alternatives is unlikely to satisfy the world's energy requirements by 2040*
- *Research into Fusion Power – which is hoped to be commercialized around 2040 – is quietly but heavily being funded by international consortia and is totally dependent on Simulation*

Molecular Biology will totally change what it means to be alive – but although it can be immensely positive it will become an ethical minefield
- *Biotechnology is being transformed by the ability to use Simulation to decide how to refine the genetic code of organisms like bacteria so as to improve their properties*
- *Genetically-Modified crops offer extraordinary benefits and most (though not all) concerns are overblown – but GM-crop take-up will still be driven by lobbying not science*
- *Animal Cloning is another emotive topic that is clouded by 'ethics experts' who can be biased by religious beliefs – but artificial human-cloning will eventually happen*

Chapter summary

- It is very likely that previously-extinct species – even woolly mammoths – will be brought back from extinction (although dinosaur DNA appears to be far too degraded)
- Stem Cell research offers the potential of life-changing therapies for everything from Alzheimer's and strokes to the replacement of defective organs such as hearts
- Genetic Therapies can reflect the unique details of an individual's DNA so as to screen for diseases, customize treatments, and potentially change unwanted genes

The net effect of Simulation with Miniaturization, Networking and Digitization will potentially lead to an unprecedented Global Renaissance

- The economics of the pharmaceutical industry mean anti-aging therapies are set dramatically to extend lifespans – some 50-year-olds today may live to 150 (or far more)
- If we can avoid the worst counter-currents to the High-Tech supertrend – some caused by its own side-effects – its impacts will overall be positive and life-affirming

ACHIEVING ESCAPE VELOCITY overview

The High-Tech supertrend is stirring up unintended consequences that risk Global Chaos rather than Global Renaissance – the general public will make the difference

- Exponentially growing High-Tech causes risky side-effects not only directly but also by stirring up five additional otherwise-benign global trends

- Boundaryless People-Power is the newly-emergent *fifth* component of the High-Tech supertrend – but unlike the others this one lets people impact the future directly

- Despite the crucial actions of governments, corporations and institutions it is the general public that ultimately will choose between Global Renaissance and Global Chaos

TURBULENCE...

...EMERGENCE...

...BOUNDARYLESS PEOPLE-POWER...

...BREAKING THE RULES...

IGNITION OF FIFTH-STAGE BOOSTER

ACHIEVING
ESCAPE VELOCITY

DARK SIDE OF THE FORCE

The combined dominance of the four established High-Tech trends makes the global economy vulnerable to any disruption to them – and each trend also causes side-effects in its own right

LET US START with the High-Tech engine itself – and then work outward through progressive zones of the turbulence it is stirring up. As you now know, the primary power that is launching the world economy into a radically new trajectory comes from the mutually-reinforcing and explosively-accelerating boosters within High-Tech. But that fact alone puts the whole launch at risk: *The combined dominance of the High-Tech trends makes the global economy vulnerable to a disruption in any of them.* If the fundamentally-exponential growth dramatically slows in areas such as computer complexity, internet size, miniaturization capability and high-capacity data-storage, then the global economy is at risk. Not only will every electronics-related business suffer, so too will every form of modern manufacturing, every trade that depends on customers buying 'the latest model', every branch of science, technology and medicine, and every institution, shareholder and pensioner that is in any way financially involved with any of those organizations.

But in addition, each of the four High-Tech trends we have already looked at stirs up major turbulence in its own right. And some of that turmoil even threatens national security. Nearly all modern forms of Digitization, for example, are highly vulnerable to technologies such as Pulse Bombs – which generate a strong electromagnetic pulse that in effect fuses computer chips. Similarly, although many risks from Networking are already well-addressed, Cyberattack remains a major threat because of the acute vulnerabilities in civilian targets. Miniaturization turbulence primarily relates to a proliferation of unaffordable healthcare options – in parallel with, as is already occurring, antibiotics failing to keep pace with emerging antibiotic-resistant strains of 'superbug' bacteria. And finally, the Simulation trend also makes biotech-design affordable to bioterrorists (as well as organized crime, for instance to create super-addictive recreational drugs) and increases the risk of accidental release of pathogens.

However, the riskiest High-Tech turbulence is that it tends to trigger unintended consequences throughout the world economy that escalate too fast for the international community to be able to respond effectively. High-Tech has become the dominant enabler of modern civilization. That means that it enhances not just opportunities – but also potential threats. As you will see across the five subchapters after this one, the most dangerous large-scale systemic risks are unintended consequences resulting from apparently-separate but actually deeply-intertwined trends. This is the indirect-turbulence caused by the High-Tech engine. And it is set to become immensely destabilizing.

THE REALITY OF GLOBAL CRISES

If you are interested in understanding the unintended consequences of High-Tech in far more depth, the material in these first six subchapters draws from the findings explained in full detail in the larger companion-volume to this book – THE REALITY OF GLOBAL CRISES: Why good beginnings are ending badly and leaving world-leaders increasingly powerless. Its book reference is ISBN-13: 978-1470115425.

These backlashes are being generated because, as a result of High-Tech, five other powerful forces embedded in global society (Capitalism, Religion, Industrialization, Population and Globalization) are starting to interact more directly and faster than ever before. The frictions that result from all these escalating interactions are stirring up unprecedented disruptions throughout the world economy. Yet the pace at which this turbulence grows is primarily driven by the exponential pace of High-Tech itself. And that means there is not the time to react that governments, and the rest of us, typically assume. The hidden threat in all of the turbulence thrown up by the High-Tech launch engine is that by the time the dangers are obvious, it is already too late. If we do not act ahead of the curve, it will be very easy for the whole international community to become progressively overwhelmed by crises.

We are better than that.

BANKERS, THE MEDIA AND POLITICIANS

Important elements of High-Tech Capitalism such as competition nevertheless cause increasingly dangerous lack of control across the world economy

CAPITALISM IS DEEPLY entrenched into global society. That means its unexpected side-effects are not only firmly established but also very complex and interconnected. The prime example of this is the inherent competition on which capitalism depends. In general, competitiveness is a very healthy component of any economy; without it, societies tend to become sluggish and outmoded because there is little pressure to improve quality of service or to innovate. But despite the crucial importance of competitiveness, when it is boosted by High-Tech it nevertheless unexpectedly introduces a set of far-reaching threats.

The addiction of many organizations to change initiatives – inspired by the lure of ever-better competitiveness, fuelled by a competitive business press and largely made possible by competitive High-Tech – is leading to widespread change-fatigue that makes it progressively harder to bring about each new change. For the last twenty years there has been an open-secret across the business community: Even under the best conditions (that is, a modern corporation) there is a 70% failure rate for major change initiatives. Government initiatives tend to be even less successful. Modern organizations are far less controllable than is generally assumed. Incessant waves of failed initiatives build further damage – typically in the form of a slowly-emerging 'change-fatigue' in which organizations potentially find each major new change initiative ever-harder to enact. If you analyze what is really going on you find that this sort of hidden change-fatigue develops not so much because employees need a break from initiative-overload but, far more insidiously, because there has built up archaeological layer upon layer of redundant or conflicting policies and procedures that increasingly restrict the freedom of an organization within a thickening straightjacket of its own history.

However, in addition to widespread potential change-fatigue, if you analyze the detail of *particular* sectors of the world economy you find a number of far-more-specific risks. For instance, another global financial crisis is inevitable because deeply-established side-effects in the banking system remain unchanged and largely unchangeable.

BANKING

I have held hundreds of one-on-one confidential discussions with banking executives around the world to decode what drives the deeply-embedded 'unwritten rules' of modern banking. In essence, the environments that most bankers work in encourage individual chronic short-termism with little regard for long-term consequences or impacts on others.

ILLUSTRATIVE BANK UNWRITTEN-RULES

"If you are a high-flyer within a typical bank then it is your immediate boss who in practice decides your bonus and defines your chances of a continued highly-paid career. And those judgments are all-too-often based only on your clearly-visible personal contribution to achieving *your boss's short-term financial performance targets*"

THEREFORE

- Keep your boss happy
- Stand out from the crowd
- Do not be seen to fail
- Protect your own turf
- Reach *short-term individual financial* targets at all costs
- Do not worry much about anything else

Although within the industry these shortcomings are well-recognized, on balance it suits banks to leave things as they are. And governments and regulators in reality have surprisingly little freedom to change the banking system without risking triggering another financial crisis as a result. Yet it was these kinds of inherent systemic risks that led to the 2008 global banking collapse. Moreover, those same systemic factors have long been encoded into not just the banking industry but also many aspect of the global economy that banking serves.

As a result, it is an extreme challenge to make constructive changes. Despite the promises of politicians, in reality, proposals such as 'bonuses paid in stock not cash' are – from everything I have uncovered – insufficient to stop individual short-term insular high-risk behavior in banks. So, until there are more radical changes, the inherent competition that High-Tech increasingly makes possible means that another global financial crash remains inevitable.

News and Politics

And then there is the impact of High-Tech competition on the News Media, and indirectly on Politics. The truth is that unintended major distortions of perception caused by how the media report stories and interact with governments are warping political control. Developments like 24/7 Rolling News unintentionally cause gross misrepresentation of the true balance of what is happening in the world. And, because the media are crucial to modern governments, those systemic distortions in reporting ultimately result in insufficient checks and balances for the political process as a whole.

Drawing again on wide-ranging confidential interviews, I have found that strong competition across the news media results in a warping of public judgment that, when combined with politics, threatens the integrity of the process by which the public chooses appropriate leaders, how politicians in turn try to manage society, and how both parties recognize what is important to be done. The recent public and political outcry against News Corporation – the world's second-largest media conglomerate – risks being just the beginning of a far more destabilizing backlash against the unintended consequences of enhanced competition within all kinds of news media, including broadcast and the internet.

Finally, there is an even more deeply hidden side-effect from High-Tech's impact on Capitalism. It links international banking, the world business community, political ideology and government. What is happening is that widespread misinterpretation of how competition optimizes the world economy risks crucially important long-term solutions being irretrievably lost.

High-Tech side-effects

The problem arises because the 'survival of the fittest' approach built into capitalism does not in any way guarantee that *over the long-term* the global economy performs well. On the contrary, capitalism is constantly culling opportunities that might be highly valuable in the long-term but are not the best local option now. Yet losing an opportunity can mean losing it forever – as is occurring in those currently-successful countries where students are being educated for types of jobs that will soon no longer exist. In the late 18th century as the Industrial Revolution took off, the backlash of unfettered Capitalism destroyed the competitiveness of whole communities as survival-of-the-fittest generally favored city economies. Some previously prosperous villages and small towns could not change fast enough and became irrelevant backwaters or simply disappeared. High-Tech combined with unfettered Capitalism risks, very slowly, doing exactly the same thing – this time with whole nations. Except, we are better than that.

How different religions react

High-Tech is inducing inevitably-escalating instabilities within some world faiths that are generating Religion side-effects that in turn destabilize everything around them

WE HAVE ALREADY seen on page 163 the turbulence caused by something like stem-cell research interacting with the more-conservative elements of certain religions. But that is just one small example of a far greater destabilization that is occurring as a result of the commotion around High-Tech. The point is that rigidity is deeply-embedded into the structure of successful world religions, making them both resilient *and* very hard to change. You might expect that when a largely-immovable object such as a long-established world Religion comes up against the largely-unstoppable force of the High-Tech launch engine there are bound to be sparks. You would be right.

Organized religions have extraordinarily well-evolved mechanisms for self-perpetuating themselves without significant change – far better than any other type of organization or institution. Given how strongly immunized against fundamental change all successful religions are, there is nothing inherently surprising in the long-standing faith-based conflicts we continue to see today. But religion-inflamed disruption is set to get significantly worse over the next few decades. The basic reason is that religions worldwide are being inexorably disrupted by High-Tech in at least four distinct ways. From all my research it appears that a combination of social changes, scientific discoveries, publicized failings in faith leadership, and wide access to conflicting insights, together have the potential rapidly to destabilize *all* religions. However, not all forms of religion are being affected equally. It appears that it is the most conservative religions that are in fact at greatest risk because the rigidity of the most *dogmatic* faiths means that they – unlike some other sects – cannot adapt but instead feel a sacred duty to push back.

High-Tech side-effects

It is High-Tech that is driving this progressive destabilization. For example, well-communicated social changes across the globe increasingly are raising alternatives that people previously were never exposed to. In parallel, exponentially-growing scientific revelation has now encroached on every area (including morals) that previously was the province of religions. Meanwhile, proliferating communication media have enabled fundamental critiquing of how religious leaders behave. And finally, well-educated believers with unprecedented informal access to historical and other evaluations of religion are increasingly confused by what they find. Taken all together, these four broadly-distinct factors are exponentially destabilizing the least-adaptable religious sects.

RESPONSES DICTATED BY RELIGIOUS PHILOSOPHY

Actions by faith leaders to bolster rigidity through intolerance and dogmatism are polarizing and politicizing – so further destabilizing – whole communities. This is because in any community, over time, professionally-organized intolerance and dogmatism tends to *dominate* over those who are informally tolerant and open-minded. Now, I am well aware that many rather-nice people (some of them good friends of mine) prefer to disbelieve that this dynamic even exists. Unfortunately, across almost three decades' analysis I have found it to be by far the most common way that a tolerant community reacts to intolerance. So, let me explain what tends to happen.

Initially, an intolerant group pulls together and voluntarily excludes itself from the wider community. But when that faction is surrounded by people who broadly tolerate it (either because they do not realize the group's views or they feel obliged to uphold free-speech and freedom of religion), the faction's goals tend to ratchet-up because there is little to constrain them. So too do the 'valid' means of achieving those goals. The more the faction feels under attack – from state-intervention, secularism, 'lowering' of moral standards, or from being labeled 'extremists' or even 'potential terrorists' – the more it feels it must push even harder. A policy of multiculturalism can enrich a community of *tolerant* and *inclusive* cultures; pursuing multiculturalism where one or more factions are inherently *intolerant* and *exclusive* inevitably leads to instability.

That is already causing problems. In particular, growing polarization caused (especially) by destabilized Christianity and Islam risks reactions that threaten the security of the whole world economy. There are many levels of granularity to the growing polarization caused by religions. But at its most abstract, some Moslem authority figures are revolted by 'Western-style depravity' that they view as an insult to Islam that must be purged, at the same time as well-organized and well-financed fundamentalist Christians are attempting to realign foreign and domestic policies around only their own exclusionist beliefs. Meanwhile, Roman Catholicism risks internal schisms that could lead to widespread social disruption.

And there are many other religious tensions growing as well, not least in the form of secular backlashes against those religious communities that are perceived as a growing threat to social coherence. Taken all together, the cumulative impact of a broadening range of increasingly-desperate religiously-inflamed resentments severely heightens the threat of widespread civil instability. In many ways, this is nobody's fault. Most individuals do not, in fact, choose their religion – it is usually chosen for them. And few if any saw the threats that would arise from High-Tech destabilizing dogmatic faiths. In that sense, until now, there is no blame. But blame does arise if, seeing what is building up, no one within or without religions does anything sufficient to calm things down. Again, we are better than that.

PEAKING OIL AND GLOBAL WARMING

High-Tech Industrialization generates two main side-effects that together threaten both the potential for Global Renaissance as well as programs to avert those threats

THE EXCEPTIONAL BENEFITS of cheap sources of concentrated energy and carbon-based chemicals have left the world-economy addicted to fossil fuels. Two-and-a-half centuries of Industrialization have led to a widespread dependency on coal, oil and natural-gas. These resources readily release large amounts of energy and can also be used to form about ten million different chemicals – including plastics, artificial fertilizers and synthetic pesticides. The continued explosion of High-Tech has *depended* on all this. However, the habit of extracting apparently-unlimited energy and chemicals generates two largely-distinct threats: Pollution side-effects and Depletion side-effects. Moreover, the impacts of those side-effects are exponential. And they are so sensitive that they are already highly politicized.

Potential responses to the first set of (pollution-related) side-effects are being deliberately undermined because, for convoluted and partially-obscured reasons, the genuine threats from climate change are being heavily misrepresented. Although the damage of local pollution from Industrialization has been obvious for centuries, the effects of airborne pollution remain far less clear-cut. With that said, it is misleading to forecast something like manmade climate-change only in terms of airborne pollution. In reality, what will happen will be the outcome of a largely-hidden conflict of incompatible goals in government, energy security, the media, private industry and oil multinationals. I have been invited in to analyze the hidden workings of all of these areas, so let me summarize my overall conclusions.

Even though a combination of politics, self-interest, complex science and unintentional media distortion is complicating interpretation of the role of Industrialization in climate-change – nevertheless, the unbiased scientific consensus is that there is an extremely high probability that manmade global warming is a genuine and serious threat to both national security and the global economy as a whole. Other interpretations are either unintentionally or (as revealed directly to me) *deliberately* being distorted.

But all the long-term crises around global warming are themselves greatly complicated by the second major Industrialization side-effect: Energy producers feel unable to publicize that production of 'cheap' forms of crude oil is peaking and costs will on-balance escalate. I have held hundreds of strictly-confidential multi-hour discussions with senior members of oil and energy companies in many countries. It has become clear that there are crucial issues broadly-recognized across the industry but not being addressed openly. The overriding unpublicized concern is that safe and cost-effective oil-production is currently peaking at a global level, with associated risks to our tightly-integrated economy.

However, because the issue of Peaking Oil is so contentious, subject to such alarmism, and clouded by so much deliberate misinformation, it is not satisfactorily reflected in international top-level negotiations regarding global warming. Any resulting agreements are therefore made based on inadequate debate of the overall trade-offs, which only makes the challenge of reducing the world-economy's addiction to oil even harder. Moreover, although governments know the security threats from climate-change and peaking oil-production, they find it close-to-impossible to change course.

There are several reasons why weaning off fossil-fuels is so hard; a very practical one is that, despite numerous proposals to lower oil-dependency and carbon-emissions, at the moment there are in reality insufficient credible alternatives that can be implemented in time to avoid many of the problems. On top of that, long-established and strongly-reinforced domestic and foreign policies tend to keep the world-economy on its current course of escalating energy costs and inadequate climate-change controls. Overall, despite excellent intentions across many government bodies, short-term local conflicting interests are currently set to undermine the very energy-focused counter-strategies that are aimed at securing long-term collective security. Surely we are better than that.

SEVEN-BILLION AND COUNTING

High-Tech combined with Population is causing side-effects that threaten extensive destabilization resulting from Competitive Overuse of resources crucial to the world economy

LARGELY THANKS TO the phenomenal benefits of High-Tech, of all those who have ever lived, 7% are alive today. Within forty years, world population is likely to rise by two billion people to reach nine billion in total. Yet that growing population – with evolving lifestyles, diets and demands – is, in effect, competing against itself for what until recently seemed like ever-renewing resources. I call this long-understood systemic pattern of runaway overexploitation of natural resources: Competitive Overuse. Losses such as rainforest and fertile topsoil are visible. Other major threats are not. For a start, global fishing power has been exploding exponentially with the result that world fish stocks are at risk of imminent collapse. By 2000, fishing fleets were extracting five times the annual catch of fifty years' before. But the average Atlantic cod that is caught today is about a third the size it was when catches were fully sustainable. Cod, haddock, Atlantic salmon and some tuna all appear to be being overfished into collapse. And governments cannot stop it.

WHEN THE CHIPS ARE DOWN

An order of 'cod and chips' may soon become a luxury. In its heyday, the largest cod used to be longer than the fisherman catching it was tall. Now it is typically less than the length of his arm. And the fish caught often are not even sexually mature, so cannot have helped replenish diminishing stocks.

ACHIEVING ESCAPE VELOCITY

The next threat triggered by Competitive Overuse is that unsustainable usage of water is leading to unprecedented risks of drought and an associated curtailment of food supplies. Massive irrigation has been crucial to feed the world. But as a result, even major rivers like the Colorado rarely make it all the way to the sea any more. Extra water is pumped up from subterranean aquifers that used to refill naturally but now often cannot keep up with demand, so countries drill deeper and extract saltier water that slowly makes land infertile. Others depend on 'fossil water' that never gets replenished. Rich nations without enough water buy food instead. But at the global level that is just a quick-fix. Fresh water is running out.

Another very different threat is revealed by the clear symptoms of early-stage failure of destabilized ecosystems crucial to many national economies. Primarily because of changes people make to habitat, extinction rates of species appear to be about a thousand times higher than historically. No one can predict the knock-on effects. As a well-documented example, collapses in colonies of bees used for agricultural pollination remain unexplained after six years' intense study. Domino-effects on agriculture of disruptions to ecosystems are now uncontrollable.

There are many other threats that arise from the massive population expansions we are seeing ultimately powered by High-Tech. Developing nations – including major countries like China and India – are at severe risk of medium-term Population-driven disruptions. Famine is as much to do with distribution of food as with availability, and it is very hard for developing nations to maintain their infrastructures in synch with rapidly-evolving populations. Population-billionaires China and India, with huge poor rural communities misaligned with fabulous urban wealth, risk local food-disruptions escalating into rebellion.

Even well-developed nations risk catastrophic destabilization in the long-term as a result of systems collapsing from unsustainable exploitation. At the same time as overpopulation is increasingly locking the global community into multiple patterns of Competitive Overuse, so national self-interest and political short-sightedness are maintaining many of the most threatening examples, ranging from unsustainable fishing quotas to unsustainable irrigation. As a result, increasing numbers of those systems that underpin the world economy are nearing an end-stage of catastrophic collapse. Yet such threats to the world economy are not driven by the actions of any nation alone, but by the uncoordinated actions of the international community as a whole. As things stand, we are unable to get our collective act together even though as a result we are all at severe risk of getting hurt. In the context of such mutual and irreparable self-harm, everyone must believe that we are better than that.

THE TUNA TEST

The Giant Bluefin Tuna is a test case as far as I am concerned. I call it my 'Tuna Test' – and I know perfectly well that if enough people choose to then our current generation will pass with flying colors. The test is simple: The international community passes the test if the Giant Bluefin Tuna survives; it gets special commendation if it thrives. The point is that, in the scheme of things, saving the Bluefin is not very important. That is why it is an important test. Saving a big fish from extinction is not likely to save a single human life. And, magnificent as it is, the Bluefin is not cute and furry like polar bears and pandas. And saving it would disrupt a number of people, not least those who fish for it. But the Tuna Test is about much more than whether as a worldwide civilization we consider it appropriate to eat another species into extinction. The far greater prize comes from demonstrating that, despite being a newly-global society, the international community is nevertheless no longer so separated, so uncoordinated, so collectively powerless – that it could not actually halt the trend even if it tried. The Tuna Test is not really the measure of how many Giant Bluefin survive. It is the measure of Humanity.

EXPLODING COMPLEXITY COMBINED WITH INTERCONNECTION

High-Tech Globalization so heightens other threats that the international community now has no mechanism to evolve effective counter-strategies against growing Global Chaos

GLOBALIZATION IS ONLY possible because of High-Tech. And yet Globalization funnels together previously largely-separate forms of turbulence in ways that are far more complex and far less understood than before. Each type of turbulence examined in the last few subchapters is affected. That includes High-Tech turbulence itself, which is further exacerbated by Globalization to enhance threats such as uncontrollable pandemics. Similarly, Globalization further stirs up the turbulence that High-Tech is already generating around Capitalism and as a result it further increases the likelihood of threats such as wild market swings, economic crashes and localized social meltdown. With Religion it enhances highly-disruptive religious schisms. With Industrialization – stirred up still more by the turbulence swirling around Capitalism – it threatens to worsen the government lack of control that unintentionally arises from the combined effect of multiple profit-driven actions taken in the multinational community (especially oil and energy suppliers as well as mining corporations).

Finally, Population turbulence exacerbated by Globalization enhances threats such as immigration 'time-bombs' exploding into civil unrest and international conflict. Taken together, each form of turbulence – as well as 'wildcard' events such as major earthquakes and tsunamis – all aggravated by Globalization, these days increasingly place the international community on near-permanent alert. Yet already political leaders struggle to cope. Contrary to popular misconception, most inadequacies in national governments and other parts of the Establishment in my experience relate far more to systems than to people. However, the hidden reality of The

System in most countries means that state-influence is increasingly difficult to exert, and anyway is misaligned with addressing complex globally-defined threats. Despite generally high competence, national government decision-making is largely unequipped to deal with globally-defined threats such as climate change or collapsing fish-stocks.

Unfortunately, supranational bodies that sit above nation states are also unsuited to exerting sufficient global governance. To be specific, in the absence of a World Government – which very few would ever want – the international community recognizes three approaches to trying to address global issues: a superpower such as the USA can adopt a philosophy that 'might is right'; clubs of nations such as the EU, NATO or the Arab League can attempt to act as one; or every recognized state can attend a forum (the United Nations) to talk with each other. All of these approaches, across numerous issues ranging from nuclear disarmament and biodiversity to fishing and global warming, are largely ineffective.

Perhaps most worrying is the failure of the UN. It is inadequate to the task because it is structured more for countries to protect local interests than global interests. Although it still works moderately well at regulating the power of individual states, the UN is trapped by its Charter into outmoded structures and voting procedures that offer little chance of reform. It cannot provide true leadership – not because of an absence of leaders but because there is no appetite for followership. All delegates feel obliged to fight for their own country's interests above all others. *None* of them fights for humanity as a whole.

CUMULATIVE TREND TOWARD GLOBAL CHAOS

The overall conclusion from analyzing the combined impact of all the interacting forms of progressively-destabilizing turbulence is that there are, at least for now, insufficient ways to devise counters to these types of globally-defined turbulence – so each country is in peril. Talks on climate-change and fishing quotas and nuclear testing do not fail because of lack of resolve, but because there is no fundamental mechanism for them to succeed. And one crisis can easily trigger another. This threatens a relentless and unstoppable cascade of potentially *all* the globally-defined crises progressively weakening the world economy and leading each nation toward a gradual but inexorable slide into increasingly destructive chaos.

This is our 'alternative' future. Despite governments' very best shots, if we do not sufficiently deal with the escalating turbulence that the High-

ACHIEVING ESCAPE VELOCITY

Tech engine is stirring up then the resultant instability will begin to stall the world economy. Governments, religions and corporations will not adapt fast enough. In an effort to resist losing the benefits of the present, key individuals will not volunteer suitable ways to make changes. They will point out politically-explosive possible implications of changing too fast. They will threaten to resign or break away if the changes impact their own community too much. And there will not be sufficiently joined-up thinking behind all the proposed actions anyway.

From everything I can forecast, the trajectory of the world economy – flattened as it already has been by the turbulence of the recent world economic crisis – is nevertheless sufficiently strong to withstand all but the worst turmoil. It will survive. But as things stand, it will not thrive. Over the next several decades, one global crisis after another then risks very slowly bringing it down. After a truly heroic struggle, the world economy would probably lose out on the chance of a Global Renaissance, and instead gradually tip toward global chaos.

Except for one thing. We are very, very much better than all that. Despite everything, I believe the world economy nevertheless really does have what it takes to get back on course. But how? After all, if even the combined might of the world's most powerful governments, corporations, religions and civil bodies still cannot break through the worst turbulence, then when and where on Earth can we possibly expect to find yet another way to boost the trajectory of our global economy sufficiently that it can achieve escape-velocity and transition into Global Renaissance?

The precise answer is around 4.40 pm, late-November, on the banks of the river Tiber in Italy.

HOW ORDER EMERGES FROM CHAOS

Although it is a term largely unknown outside science, Emergence is a well-understood process that can solve what is otherwise impossibly detailed and localized.

IN LATE AUTUMN huge flocks of starlings gather at dusk over Rome. They swirl through the sky with such breathtaking coordination that they appear like an impossibly large shawl of gossamer-silk drifting on the breeze above the city. If a bird of prey attacks, the flock splits and reforms according to a hugely sophisticated choreography; the shawl miraculously repairs itself and becomes whole again. It is one of the most awe-inspiring spectacles of nature. And it is all an illusion. *There are no coordinated flocks.*

EMERGENCE, CHAOS AND COMPLEXITY

'Emergence' is a crucial discovery that comes from the field of Complexity Theory – a discipline that itself evolved from Chaos Theory (which in turn came out of Cybernetics, which is where long ago I first became familiar with the concepts as a research student). Chaos Theory and Complexity Theory are, in effect, viewing the spectrum of systems that occur in everyday existence from opposite ends of that spectrum. Chaos Theory explains how apparently-random behavior can be generated by systems that are only following completely non-random rules; counterintuitively, some precisely-defined set ups can nevertheless progress in completely unpredictable ways. Complexity Theory comes at reality from the other direction. It explains how some immensely-complicated behavior – such as evolution, human-consciousness and AI, or the apparently-coordinated flocking behavior of starlings – can in fact arise from very-simple rules.

ACHIEVING ESCAPE VELOCITY

There are only thousands of individual birds with no leader and no plan. They have not all adopted an Aerial Display Strategy. They do not have a Chief Flocking Officer. Each bird is acting completely autonomously. Yet the behavior of the flock remains wholly astounding. It is as close to Magic as science can ever attempt to comprehend. Even when the hidden mechanism behind the illusion is decoded, still there is no trick – the inner-workings of the mystery, once revealed, remain equally magical.

In science we call the phenomenon 'Emergence': wonderfully sophisticated order that under the right conditions materializes out of apparent chaos. In the case of the starlings, it is caused by each bird instinctively trying to stay as close as possible to its neighbors without touching. That almost trivial rule, when it is replicated across *every* bird, translates into a complexity of behavior that mirrors Intelligence. Such 'distributed intelligence' can sometimes overcome apparently insurmountable obstacles. The rise of human civilization is peppered with examples of this sort of emergent problem solving.

EMERGENCE AND DISCOVERING CHEDDAR CHEESE

To make Cheddar Cheese: Use cow's milk, but only when it is coming out thinner than usual, then add Rennet (found in the fourth stomach of a suckling calf – if the calf is weaned, it is less effective). Only if the milk is warmed to above normal room temperature will it then split into sludge (curds) and liquid (whey), otherwise nothing happens. If successful, the result smells rather like baby-sick. Very slowly comb the curds and then leave everything alone. You can pour the whey off and feed it to your animals, break the curds up, add some salt, press the result, and you will get a cheese that lasts about a month. If instead you reheat the whey and add it again to the curds, that process of 'cheddaring' the cheese means that it will last six-to-eight months. Given that no one knew that the concept of Cheddar Cheese even existed, and many of the intermediate steps are rather unappetizing, the only way that this extraordinarily-complex recipe was ever discovered was Emergence. Over maybe thousands of years, myriad happy-accidents and failed attempts at storing food eventually led to a recipe that worked better than all the others. And everyone copied it.

Boundaryless People-Power

Throughout history and around the world, it is Emergence that has in fact been the mechanism by which humanity made collective breakthroughs that no individual or small group controlled. To this day it is Emergence that creates the relative order of Markets – whether in an ancient village square or across ultra-modern global financial exchanges. And it is Emergence that has just finished constructing what appears to be a previously-invisible *fifth-stage* booster to the world economy. That booster, it turns out, is yet another component of the High-Tech engine; it potentially exerts one of the most powerful forces the world has ever seen.

THE FIFTH-STAGE BOOSTER

There is a growing form of Emergence across electronically-linked like-minded individuals that spontaneously creates Boundaryless People-Power

TRIGGERED BY AN unplanned mix of 24/7 internet traffic, mobile-phone video, instant messaging, Skype, Twitter, yfrog, Flickr, Facebook, viral YouTube clips, blogs, on-line archived data, Google, the ubiquity of Microsoft, virtual reality, simulations of unviewable phenomena, global news-networks, TV phone-voting, citizen journalism, pressure groups, lack of faith in the Establishment, widespread concern about the future, belief in the impact of peaceful protest – there is emerging an embryonic phenomenon that shows the characteristics of globally-interlinked 'community action' amplified by unprecedented awareness. I think of it as Boundaryless People-Power.

Billions of people are tying into something that more than ever before not only links them across Space but also, because they can equally-readily access other people's thoughts generated seconds or centuries earlier, across Time as well. An entity like it has never existed before. Fed by the explosive components of the High-Tech supertrend and of, amongst others, the Globalization, Population and Capitalism trends, its power is growing exponentially. And that looks like changing everything.

This new phenomenon is already behaving as if it had a mind of its own – although it certainly does not have a consciousness or anything like it, any more than a flock of starlings has. Moreover, no institution is in control of (or even initially aware of) the emergent behavior any more than any individual starling is in control of, or aware of, the magnificence displayed above Rome. But Boundaryless People-Power has started to have a profound yet complex impact on global society. Highly-visible examples have been the viral-spread of reports by citizen-journalists of civil-demonstrations resulting in immediate international reaction that changes the effectiveness and spread of the demonstrations themselves, as happened in the Arab Spring of 2011 with the spread of unrest from Tunisia to Egypt to much of the Middle-East.

EMERGENT CONSCIOUSNESS OF THE INTERNET

Despite what many forecasters have suggested, it is not at all clear whether even a highly advanced form of the internet – linking in as it would many AI systems that might individually claim to have self-awareness – could ever exhibit any form of 'consciousness' itself. After all, humans in a close-knit group still just remain humans. However, that may simply be because we can only communicate with each other very inefficiently (in comparison with the networked neurons in our brains or, indeed, networked computers). Suffice to say, any supernet consciousness would likely be very alien and quite possibly, at least initially, completely unrecognizable.

Like all forms of Emergence, the detail of what Boundaryless People-Power does is necessarily unpredictable. But there is something highly-unusual about the overall pattern of how this particular phenomenon works. Unlike the other four stages of the High-Tech engine or the turbulence they stir up – all of which are in practice impossible to control – Boundaryless People-Power not only can potentially be influenced directly, but it also has the power to *counter global turbulence directly*. That sounds ridiculous, but the reason it has so much potential impact is that it increasingly taps into everything and everyone. And that is exactly what is needed to streamline the world economy.

LEGACY EFFECTS

At the moment the international community is stuck with all kinds of Legacy Effects – processes and systems that maybe worked well in the past (or at least their downsides were less obvious) but that now are causing friction. Some Legacy Effects manifest themselves as fundamental instabilities within regional economies or social groupings or crucial infrastructures that politicians dare not confront. Others persist as knowingly-inappropriate relationships between journalists, politicians and the police. Some show themselves as escalating religion-inspired conflict. Others find us hunting natural food supplies into extinction at the same time as depleting other unsustainable natural resources. But all of the Legacy Effects that cause undue friction are now a threat.

ACHIEVING ESCAPE VELOCITY

Legacy Effects are ultimately only kept in place by the combination of beliefs, habits, styles, traditions, etiquette, policies, procedures, rules and laws that people hang onto. The grip of that mishmash can be almost unbreakable. As a result, over many centuries it has become increasingly difficult for humanity as a whole deliberately to make radical changes to the course it is on, primarily because so many of the inner-workings of civilization have gradually become dominated by Legacy Effects from the past.

HOW DESTINY STACKS THE DECK

Despite everyone having Free Will, important strands of our future nevertheless get disconcertingly close to being Pre-ordained. It is rather like when a conjuror spreads out a genuine pack of playing cards with the words: 'Pick a card, any card.' Even though we can select whichever card we like, the most likely future may be that we pick out a numbers card that is a Diamond. Why? Well, for a start, we are far more likely to want to choose a card from somewhere around the middle of the pack rather than from either end. And if any card is sticking out from the pack we will probably avoid it.

Those two common decisions are completely ours to make, but we are already voluntarily cutting down our options. If, unknown to us, the conjuror has stacked the deck so the middle cards are all Diamonds then the outcome of our genuinely free choice is suddenly a lot less open. If in addition the conjuror has managed to get the Jack, Queen and King of Diamonds slightly to stick out of the pack, then the most likely future, for most people, most of the time, will be to pick a numbers card that is a Diamond. Yet each person has a completely free choice.

That is how 'Destiny' works. Our deck is *always* stacked. In our everyday world, the type of choices we have to make, the options that are available to us, the information and approaches by which we make up our minds are in practice all dominated by the combined impact of the last 5000 years of human history. And that is what stacks the deck.

Boundaryless People-Power

For five thousand years, since people first formed cities, the progress of civilization has increasingly been driven – and constrained – by the accumulated actions of those who came before us. Important contributory drivers of our future have effectively been left to us by our ancestors. Handed down across two-hundred generations, we have inherited the ultimate legacy. And as part of it, the major trends that already largely dictate our lives (some of which have been the focus of this book) are inextricably embedded into almost every aspect of how the modern world operates.

That raises a vital question: If all the formal and informal rules that hold today's world economy together also conspire to keep many aspects acting broadly in the same long-established ways – whether Industrialization or Capitalism or Religion – how can we ever hope to deliberately change the course of history? How can we dream of a new beginning if Destiny always has the cards stacked so heavily in favor of the status quo? How can we conceivably win a better future than we have been dealt if the rules mean we cannot even change our cards?

To achieve that, like all those who have ever succeeded in deliberately changing the future, we need to do something wonderfully human. We need to break the rules. In a coordinated and deliberate way we need to use Boundaryless People-Power to break the formal and informal rules that keep the most damaging Legacy Effects in place.

BREAKING THE RULES

To be fair, various communities have been experimenting with highly-constrained forms of Boundaryless People-Power for some time. They used it to change the future when raw people-power – stimulated by international media-coverage – ripped aside the Iron Curtain, made fur unfashionable, banned most whaling, and forced various overhauls of national politics (even expense-claims in the Mother of Parliaments at Westminster). But its capabilities were very limited. People never had the collective power to address the really-big issues. Nor did they have the means to build momentum across much of the global community. That is changing.

Boundaryless People-Power already directly ties into those who are unintentionally maintaining the self-imposed restraints that hold the world-economy on its current track (such as the pressures to keep depleting certain non-renewable resources). That is what gives this unique phenomenon its power to reduce globally-defined frictions directly. In theory, for example, everyone could simply stop eating an endangered species such as the sushi-delicacy Giant Bluefin Tuna, and just like that, the species would be saved. Although that is an unusually simple pattern of solution (probably neither more nor less likely than when fashionable people stopped wearing mink), the reality remains that when large numbers of people 'break the rules' and change their behavior all in much the same way, the future of the global economy changes from what otherwise would have occurred.

Deliberately achieving that sort of shift is far from trivial though. We must not be naive about just how untamed Boundaryless People-Power currently is. Although some people glamorize the notion of the collective-intelligence of vast numbers of relative strangers all linked together as one, in reality the social dynamics can quick as a flash turn into those of a lynch mob. Anonymous crowds can all-too-easily turn against the very people they previously adored; the deposed leaders of every failed revolution in history are examples of that, and the global community is no more forgiving today. People have too little time. Crowd emotions are too readily swayed.

As an example, many of us still remember the tremendous sympathy and outpouring of grief throughout the world that followed the tragic death of Princess Diana after her car sped through a Parisian road-tunnel and crashed into a concrete pillar. Imagine how the worldwide public might have reacted instead if the news media had, in an alternative future, reported that Diana and her superrich Arab lover had remained completely unharmed within their luxury limousine – but three of the young French lads following them on bikes had been killed by their drunken chauffeur swerving into them. Boundaryless People-Power is not automatically a benign or consistent force, any more than each of us as individuals is.

As a result, we need to be very respectful of our new superpower. But, even given such healthy caution, it is fair to say that this fifth-stage booster nevertheless has *immense* potential. To a large extent it is fuelled directly by High-Tech, so it will increasingly be strong enough to take on anything. What is more, Boundaryless People-Power has the ability to trigger harmonized behavior-changes that counter specific turbulences directly. *And it is all of us that collectively steer Boundaryless People-Power.*

THE BIRTHRIGHT OF EVERY HUMAN-BEING

Boundaryless People-Power can change the future by enough people 'breaking the rules' that otherwise hold them on course – and also agreeing what *not* to change

TO SHOW YOU why the emergence of Boundaryless People Power is almost unimaginably significant, I need to set it within a bit of historical context: 13.7-billion years ago there was a Big Bang, then a *really* big gap. For an interminably long time the universe was incredibly boring; magnificent, but fundamentally mind-numbing. Earth finally formed, there was a huge collision and we got our moon. Lots of volcanoes followed, then water, simple life, oxygen, complex life. But even after the Cambrian explosion (when life-forms became really interesting) the inner workings of our future remained surprisingly dull. Things just happened. 65-million years ago the dinosaurs could not avoid extinction as a result of meteorite strikes any more than humans could 75-thousand years ago when they were almost wiped out by a supervolcano. They were all powerless. Their future just rolled over them. Until around 5,000 years ago.

People call it the Dawn of Civilization. But it is *so* much more. It is the moment the structure of the future becomes fascinating – because for the first time humankind successfully rebelled against Destiny. Cave dwellers could try to impact their individual lives. But they could not deliberately change the course of history for all humans in the way that, say, the ancient Egyptians did. Those first civilizations showed it was possible for a single individual occasionally to make such a difference that it affected everybody who followed. From the moment of that great divide in history, *it became the birthright of every human-being to be able to change the future.*

ACHIEVING ESCAPE VELOCITY

That Brief History of the Universe is the context in which Boundaryless People-Power is now emerging. Only for the last five millennia have leaders formed substantial organizations around themselves to help fundamentally change the future in the ways they wanted. Even today, as lone individuals we struggle to make any difference, but surrounded by the right people – and branded as Microsoft or Greenpeace or The White House – an individual can, very rarely, change the future of the whole planet. And yet now, for the *very, very first time* in 13.7-billion years (at least in this sector of the galaxy) a mechanism is growing by which almost everyone throughout our world community can act together to influence its future directly. Indeed, enough people can now come together to 'break the rules' of pretty well any aspect of our global existence. In many ways the individual skills that are required seem trivial. Even children can deliberately break the rules, and society often acts as if it is something to be ashamed of. In reality, it may be civilization's greatest gift.

Only humans Break the Rules. Other advanced primates have grammar, can tell lies, they suffer from depression, use tools, demonstrate complex learning abilities and they plan for the long term. But only people deliberately break the rules – or choose not to. Breaking the rules is the breathtaking attribute that more than any other has powered the ascent of civilization. It is a uniquely human balancing act of self-serving creativity matched with altruistic restraint, of audacious implementation with intuitive risk-assessment. In a crucial sense this trait defines both our species and our society: Deliberately breaking the rules is what makes us human; agreeing which rules we choose *not* to break is what makes us civilized.

Our generation is the first, ever, in the inconceivably long history of this part of the universe, to be granted the opportunity to prove our mastery of selectively Breaking the Rules on a planetary scale, and in so doing, to rewrite our global future. In truth, it is not a challenge we can refuse any longer. It is time to make a difference.

Making a difference

Despite the crucial actions of governments, corporations and institutions it is the general public that ultimately will choose between Global Renaissance and Global Chaos

WE FEEL LOCKED on our current risky trajectory because so many of the trends that drive the global economy, and consequently stir up turbulence, are tightly bonded into everyday life. Whether it is widespread addiction to the one-off energy-boost from fossil-fuels or the seeming-inevitability of one religion fighting another or countries' apparent powerlessness to avoid slaughtering a species to extinction, we feel we cannot break free. But like the existence of a coordinated flock of starlings – it is all an illusion. The strongest bonds that bind the global economy on its high-risk course ultimately exist nowhere but collectively in our heads.

That is not to say that barriers in people's heads are not sometimes extremely strong. If able-bodied individuals were asked if they could walk, without losing their balance, along a line that was a bit wider than their feet, few of them would have any hesitation in saying they could, even if the wind was blowing quite strongly. So, there is absolutely no reason why they could not do exactly the same on an equally-wide beam stretching between two skyscrapers. The difference is in their heads.

When a society makes a major choice, it can often feel like walking out on a high beam. Centuries ago, the abolition of slavery cost countries dear. Economically it did not appear to make sense. Those who fought against the idea put up innumerable barriers to reform. At times, those barriers seemed insurmountable. Yet nevertheless, one society after another abolished slavery basically because they decided it was the right thing to do – even if sometimes it was also because they saw slave-owners as having an unfair competitive advantage against those who had to pay their workers. Enough people wrestled with their consciences and came to the conclusion that they no longer wanted to be part of such a fundamental breach of human rights. Some of them also concluded that it was in their long-term enlightened self-interest. But the outcome was the same. Ultimately, enough people making the same decision overcame all the barriers. It should have been no surprise. In truth, people changing their minds had been the only barriers to reform that had *ever* existed.

In many ways, the recognition that so many 'insurmountable barriers' to realigning the trajectory of the world economy are in fact only inside our heads is a liberating thought. However unlikely it may seem for people collectively to break free from the tide of turbulence that currently is drifting us toward global chaos, it is completely in our power to do so. When it really comes down to it, it is a choice. And symptoms of the early-phases of that selection process are already beginning to be seen in everything from the Arab Spring triggered in Tunisia to the backlash against invasions of privacy by the press triggered in the UK.

WHERE TOMORROW COMES FROM

The impact of Boundaryless People-Power is set to spread. The sophistication of its coordinated actions is set to grow. Its shared wisdom is set to increase. This is not primarily a social phenomenon; it is at its core a High-Tech phenomenon. And that means that it is set to balloon in power, just like the other four components of the High-Tech engine. By 2040, its reach will not be the equivalent of an arm's length. It will be further than the orbit of Mars.

That is why Boundaryless People-Power will add a fifth-stage to the launch engine that is propelling global progress. And it is why this emerging fifth-stage has the power to determine whether, despite all the turbulence we are causing, the world economy can nevertheless maintain a sufficient trajectory to escape the pull of the past. By participating in the emergent phenomenon of Boundaryless People-Power, informal leaders throughout society, many of them apparently just 'ordinary' members of the general public, will increasingly *make a difference*. And if enough people break the right legacy-rules but leave society's more productive rules intact, then the fifth-stage Booster will indeed prove sufficient to break free from the worst Legacy Effects that are causing such escalating friction.

Sometimes, at the individual level, it will not feel easy. It is always daunting to take a decision to act on something that is so fundamental and so complicated that it seems like an impossibly-overwhelming challenge. But in the Theatre of Civilization, numerous heroes and heroines across

Making a difference

history have risen to the challenge of playing a starring role. Our generation will be no different. When Rosa Parks refused to give up her seat to make room for a white passenger on a public bus, when the drag queens stood up to police-intimidation at the Stonewall gay club, when Emmeline Pankhurst fought for women's rights, when Gandhi began his Salt March for independence, when that first unnamed person hit the first sledgehammer against the first slab of the Berlin Wall – those individuals each claimed their birthright to improve the future. The next Act is ours.

Tomorrows mainly come from yesterdays. And the legacies of previous generations can unknowingly trap us on a dangerous course. It is easy then to rant against the unfairness of what we have inherited. That is how many of our predecessors lived and died – unable in practice to escape the dangers created by those who came before them, any more than they could avoid passing onto their children the buried seeds of crises yet to develop. For two-hundred generations that has been the pattern of the future. But *our* tomorrow must be different because it is our generation that must leave the most important legacy of all. For the first time, humanity has the power either to destroy itself or fundamentally to transform itself into something extraordinary. By the sum of our actions and inactions we will either be submerged into a global chaos distilled from short-termism and insularity, or we will triumphantly break through into Global Renaissance.

The next few decades are when many of the repeating patterns of five-thousand years of human civilization need to adapt. And it is we alone who can achieve that. Ultimately this is our time, our choice, our future because, thanks to the emergence of Boundaryless People-Power, it is each of us that is now contributing to our fate. Global Renaissance or Global Chaos? It is all of us who will make that collective choice. Together we elect our own destiny. Our tomorrow does not only come from yesterday. The reality of our global future is that an important part of tomorrow comes from *You*.

ACHIEVING ESCAPE VELOCITY

The High-Tech supertrend is stirring up unintended consequences that risk Global Chaos rather than Global Renaissance – the general public will make the difference

Exponentially growing High-Tech causes risky side-effects not only directly but also by stirring up five additional otherwise-benign global trends

- *The combined dominance of the four established High-Tech trends makes the global economy vulnerable to any disruption to them – and each trend also causes side-effects in its own right*
- *Important elements of High-Tech Capitalism such as competition nevertheless cause increasingly dangerous lack of control across the world economy*
- *High-Tech is inducing inevitably-escalating instabilities within some world faiths that are generating Religion side-effects that in turn destabilize everything around them*
- *High-Tech Industrialization generates two main side-effects that together threaten both the potential for Global Renaissance as well as programs to avert those threats*
- *High-Tech combined with Population is causing side-effects that threaten extensive destabilization resulting from Competitive Overuse of resources crucial to the world economy*
- *High-Tech Globalization so heightens other threats that the international community now has no mechanism to evolve effective counter-strategies against growing Global Chaos*

Chapter summary

Boundaryless People-Power is the newly-emergent *fifth* component of the High-Tech supertrend – but unlike the others this one lets people impact the future directly

- *Although it is a term largely unknown outside science, Emergence is a well-understood process that can solve what is otherwise impossibly detailed and localized*
- *There is a growing form of Emergence across electronically-linked like-minded individuals that spontaneously creates Boundaryless People-Power*
- *Boundaryless People-Power can change the future by enough people 'breaking the rules' that otherwise hold them on course – and also agreeing what not to change.*

Despite the crucial actions of governments, corporations and institutions it is the general public that ultimately will choose between Global Renaissance and Global Chaos

ACKNOWLEDGEMENTS

Over my career I have had six books published by well-respected firms. To be fair, until very recently that was the only credible track for a serious author to take. But the traditional route costs – figuratively and literally. Old-style publishing is about sales volume and price. However successful your earlier books, editors encourage you to write what they think 'the market' wants (more accurately, what book-distributors think they want based on a twelve-word description) rather than the message *you* want to convey to a possibly more-specialized readership. And when it comes to truly affordable eBook editions, publishers can seem a little reluctant.

What is more, over the last decade a form of laziness has crept into the industry: Except for those of us lucky enough to have worked with them already, large publishing houses typically now only consider new book ideas that are brought to them by Literary Agents rather than proposed directly by authors. Most publishers will not even accept direct submissions, so new authors have become progressively excluded from the complex decision-making that determines the market and marketing of intellectual capital. New ideas can too easily be stifled. Just as happened in the pop-music industry, book publishers became a bit too comfortable.

As I got into writing this book (about The Future, after all) I increasingly realized I had little enthusiasm to submit myself once again to a publishing process based on little more than a computerized upgrade of a nineteenth-century business model. It felt archaic and long-overdue for radical overhaul. And then, bang on schedule, along came Amazon and Kindle. I am immensely grateful to all of the gang – not just those who have helped me directly but also everyone that is ensuring that a new publishing mindset will become part of the reality of our global future.

I am, as ever, indebted to my confidential corporate, institutional and private clients around the world who since the 1980s have provided me with the otherwise inaccessible insights on which this book is based. Also to my numerous colleagues and pupils along the way who have acted as caring but critical audiences on which to test my thinking. Finally, love goes to my always-supportive family and friends and above all, as in each of my previous books, to my partner for the last third of a century, Francis.

Thanks to *everyone* who has helped make Global Future a Reality.

INDEX

Index

Index

ABOUT THE AUTHOR

As foremost authority on the hidden inner-workings of the world economy, Dr. Peter B Scott-Morgan has been invited to decode the complex reality behind all the main components of the international community. For more than 25 years and across the USA, Europe, Asia Pacific and Latin America he has been offered exceptional access to institutions, government organizations and corporations (including many of the major players in banking, pharmaceuticals, oil, energy, IT, telecoms and media) to analyze their systemic threats and advise their leaders how to respond. He is one of very few that has ever gained so much confidential insight into such a wide-ranging sample of the world economy.

Dr. Scott-Morgan has given more than a thousand speeches, presentations and workshops in over thirty countries and has spent approximately the same amount of his career based in the USA as in Europe. He has an expert knowledge of technology, sociology and management science, and a detailed grasp of history and politics. With specialist expertise in system dynamics, organizational strategy and change management he has built a track record of published thought-leadership, authoring over a hundred articles and refereed papers, as well as several reference materials and six books.

Within academia he has taught numerous post-graduate MBA courses in London, Boston and Rotterdam, as well as been Professor of Business and Chairman of the Board of Trustees at a Boston-based international Business School. In corporate life he has been Senior Vice President of a 3,500-person professional-services firm and the Managing Director of a 150-person international management consultancy.